BETTING ON LEFTY

*The True Story of Frank Rosenthal
and the Mafia in Las Vegas*

MAFIA LIBRARY

© **Copyright 2024 - All rights reserved.**

The content contained within this book may not be reproduced, duplicated or transmitted without direct written permission from the author or the publisher.

Under no circumstances will any blame or legal responsibility be held against the publisher, or author, for any damages, reparation, or monetary loss due to the information contained within this book, either directly or indirectly.

Legal Notice:

This book is copyright protected. It is only for personal use. You cannot amend, distribute, sell, use, quote or paraphrase any part, or the content within this book, without the consent of the author or publisher.

Disclaimer Notice:

Please note the information contained within this document is for educational and entertainment purposes only. All effort has been executed to present accurate, up to date, reliable, complete information. No warranties of any kind are declared or implied. Readers acknowledge that the author is not engaged in the rendering of legal, financial, medical or professional advice. The content within this book has been derived from various sources. Please consult a licensed professional before attempting any techniques outlined in this book.

By reading this document, the reader agrees that under no circumstances is the author responsible for any losses, direct or indirect, that are incurred as a result of the use of the information contained within this document, including, but not limited to, errors, omissions, or inaccuracies.

TABLE OF CONTENTS

Introduction 1

Chapter 1 : Chicago Kid 13
    Playing The Ponies 13
    A Born Gambler 16

Chapter 2 : The Fix Is In 27
    The Chicago Outfit 28
    Tony The Ant 37

Chapter 3 : "The Bookies Go To Florida And The Players Eat Snowballs..." 45
    Trouble In The 1960s 46
    Moving To Miami 52

Chapter 4 : Viva Mob Vegas 61
    An Oasis In The Desert 62
    A Match Made In Vegas 70

Chapter 5 : A Hole In The Wall 79
    A Little Off The Top 80
    The Gold Rush 87

Chapter 6 : High Times At The Stardust 93
    Time To Settle Down? 93
    "That's A Good-Looking Ten Of Spades..." 96
    Not A Normal Man 103

Chapter 7 : A Snake With Two Heads 109
    For The Benefit Of Others 109
    The Great Innovator 114

Chapter 8 : The Rosenthal Show 121
    Getting Famous 122
    The Dry Snitch 126

Chapter 9 : Crashing Down 131
    Tony, Frank, And Geri 131
    Glick's Downfall 138
    The 1981 El Dorado 142

Conclusion : Codename Achilles 155

References 163

INTRODUCTION

In the 1960s, Las Vegas was a city of grand and beautiful neon lights, marquee signs bright enough to replace daylight itself, and flashy, luxurious lifestyles. It was the place where dreams came true and where dreams were shattered. It was a playground for men and women across the world who wanted to indulge in the guilty pleasures that they simply couldn't get anywhere else. Legal gambling, of course, was its most enticing attraction. Home to beautiful, towering casinos and luxury hotels, Vegas had become in just a few decades the world capital of gambling all your money away. It was also a town that favored efficiency, even when it came to love: Americans from around the country had for years flocked to Las Vegas, a veritable oasis in the middle of a barren desert, to get married in just a few hours without all the hassle and bureaucratic red tape that their own state's government demanded. But, just like the fortunes of those who gambled their life savings away at the blackjack tables, love vanished as quickly as it came. Vegas was there to service that need too, and quickly became the divorce capital of America.

Las Vegas was also a city of crime. The massive draw of the city's gambling culture and the relatively lax attitude of the Las Vegas Metro police presented plenty of opportunities for criminals of all stripes. Card sharks, scammers, loan sharks, pimps and prostitutes, drug pushers, illegal bookies, and thieves all made Las Vegas their home from the 1940s onwards. On the Vegas strip, you could walk into almost any building and find a table to win a few thousand dollars, then lose twice that an hour later. A drug binge was just a conversation away and spending the night with a lady (or several) was simply a matter of price point. Any vice you could imagine was always within arm's reach in this city, so long as you knew where to look. It was a haven for good vibes and bad habits, and criminals both big and small were behind almost all of it. Without a doubt though, the number one criminal enterprise in the city belonged to the Families of the Italian-American Mafia.

The Mafia had long dominated the American criminal underworld, and the cities that they called home felt the effects of this. In big cities like New York City, Chicago, Philadelphia, Boston, Detroit, Los Angeles, and elsewhere, gangland killings and turf wars between Families were commonplace. A city like Vegas, where billions of dollars flowed through the casinos each year, was ripe for the Families that were looking to expand their territory. Indeed, Mafia involvement in the casino business is about as old as the city of Vegas itself. But there, in the blinding light of the Vegas Strip, crime was different. There were no Mafia bloodbaths, no violent turf wars, and what murders there were usually stayed out of the headlines and out of the public eye. Las Vegas was an "open city," a place where Mafia Families from across the country could move in and set up business without needing the express permission of other Families. None of the Families "owned" Vegas, and no one needed to pay tributes to operate there. The Las Vegas casinos, many of which were owned by Mafia Families from Chicago and other mid western cities, were absolute cash cows for the Mafia, and no one wanted to risk their golden goose by drawing attention to their operations. Peaceful co-existence was the name of the game, and so long as Vegas police were willing to look the other way, spectacles of violence and mob wars were off the table.

Even small-time criminals had little to fear from the Mafia. After all, why bother wasting time extorting cash from a petty pill pusher when the real cash was in the casino counting rooms? So, for decades Vegas provided a kind of safe space for both criminals and average people. If mobsters let crime affect the lives of tourists, then tourists would stop showing up to feed their slot machines and spin their roulette wheels. It was in the best interest of everyone to uphold Las Vegas' clean reputation, so when 1970 rolled around, "Sin City" was certainly sinful, but at least it was not particularly dangerous. But, in the span of less than a decade, all of that was over. The city had utterly transformed, and Las Vegas had become home to brutal gangsters and armed robbers who had no issue killing whoever got in their way. The city where both big and small criminals could operate freely was now being terrorized by vicious thugs looking to dominate the city's underworld and turn Vegas' free market of crime into a strict fiefdom where everyone paid tribute to the big man at the top. The main prize, of course, was total control over the city's multimillion-dollar casino industry.

The main question, of course, is how this came to be. How did Las Vegas become such a scene for murder, and how did its streets become so infested with violence and thuggery? Both in and outside of the casinos, most things in this city ultimately boiled down to gambling, and all the vices that came with it. Of course, gambling was not a new invention, and Las Vegas was certainly not the first city to feel the impact of gambling. In fact, the very act of gambling seems to be much older than recorded human history. Some of the oldest texts in existence make reference to betting for cash, and both the Old and New Testaments of the Bible mention the sins and degeneracy of gambling for money. Even in ancient Greek mythology, the gods are said to have played games of chance to determine certain aspects of the world. Needless to say, gambling is an itch that has needed scratching since human civilization first took shape.

Importantly for this story, the history of gambling and sports has also always gone hand-in-hand. The Olympic Games date back to around the 700s BC. The Roman Colosseum held grand sporting events thousands of years ago. In both Greece and Rome, placing bets on these games was extremely common, and it is the main reason that the depictions of rabid, cheering hordes at the Colosseum are so similar to the ones seen at horse racing tracks even today. In Rome, chronic gambling addiction became so rampant that Emperor Augustus had to restrict betting to a single week of the calendar year. But gambling wasn't the only thing they were doing. Long before the extravagance and flashy lights of Las Vegas, criminal exploitation was a staple in sports and gambling. Around 338 BC, the Thessalian boxer Eupolus was discovered to have paid several of his opponents to throw their fights against him during the Olympics. This trend carried well into modern history. After the formation of major sports leagues in America, a new age of gambling and corruption dawned. The National League, a pro baseball organization, formed in 1876 and it took only a single year for one team, the Louisville Grays, to get caught up in a massive bet fixing scandal. Later, in 1921, the commissioner of American baseball was forced to issue total sports bans to eight Chicago White Sox players that were found to have conspired to intentionally throw the 1919 World Series for their team.

In the 1950s, crooked sports betting reached even more shocking heights with the 1951 scandal at City College in New York. CCNY was the school most heavily implicated in the scandal, but it ultimately involved dozens of players across seven national school teams. These players had successfully been bribed to shave points (essentially, missing scores on purpose) off of over 80 basketball games in the space of four years, a revelation that shook the sporting world. But who could be behind such massive sports fixing operations? Surely it wasn't the teams themselves, nor was it the small-time gamblers who were placing the bets with their bookies. In almost all of the cases like this, it was mobsters and organized criminals pulling the strings and greasing the palms of the players and coaches. Gambling has always been a lucrative part of the American Mafia's illegal income, and this has been especially true with sports betting. In 1978, two infamous Lucchese Family associates, Henry Hill and James Burke (who were both subjects of the 1990 Martin Scorsese film *Goodfellas*) spearheaded an operation to bribe several college players to fix games that their mob bookies had odds on. Their methods were a bit more advanced, though. Rather than just having the players lose the game, they wanted them to create a very specific point differential so that as few players as possible would beat the "spread," essentially meaning the margin of victory the winning team has. These point spreads were set by the mob bookies themselves, and then it was up to the players to make sure the mob minimized how much they had to pay out.

To be able to craft the perfect odds for the most profit, it took a very special mind. It took someone who saw sports and odds and chance like no one else did. It took someone who dedicated himself to reading statistics and analyzing trends. For the Chicago branch of the American Mafia, also known as the Chicago Outfit, that man was none other than Frank Rosenthal, and he was the best at doing it, ever. For well over a decade, Rosenthal was widely believed to have been the best sports handicapper in the entire United States. From childhood, Rosenthal had a keen eye for everything that had to do with odds, especially when it came to who was going to hit a game-winning home run and which team was bound for the college championship. Having grown up and spent most of his life around some of the most notorious members of Chicago's criminal underworld, no one valued his talents more than the Outfit. In return for their faith in him, Rosenthal made them an absolute fortune over the course of several decades. There were plenty of guys all around the country looking to beat the system and make the unpredictable act of gambling a "sure thing." But, without a doubt, no one did it like Frank Rosenthal, or as his mobster friends affectionately referred to him, "Lefty."

Lefty turned out to be useful for more than fixing games and optimizing the odds. He was also a brilliant, meticulous manager of resources who the top gangsters in Chicago entrusted with running operations worth hundreds of millions of dollars. The young Jewish kid from the streets of Chicago's West Side who grew up around thugs and gangsters eventually, at his peak, was running a total of four of Las Vegas' most glamorous and profitable casinos and hotels. Lefty's impact on these casinos, all of which were bankrolled and backed by the Chicago Outfit, earned the Mafia bosses more money than they ever could have dreamt of making through backroom poker games and small-time bookmaking.

When he first arrived in Las Vegas in the late 1960s, his feet were not nearly the first set of feet planted in that city by the Mafia. Mobsters had been making a killing off gambling rings for well over a century by that point, so it's no surprise that they had also been involved in the Las Vegas scene since the city first became the mecca for the country's slots players, craps shooters, high rollers, and degenerates.

It was infamous mob guys like Bugsy Siegel and Meyer Lansky who walked in Las Vegas so that Frank "Lefty" Rosenthal could run. One of the very first modern casinos in the city, the "Fabulous Flamingo," was founded by Siegel in 1946. Siegel had already fallen in love with the city because of the state of Nevada's uniquely loose gambling regulations, and after securing over a million dollars financed by his Mafia connections in New York City, he set out to create a glamorous resort-style casino for gamblers of all stripes. The same year the Flamingo debuted, Guy McAfee, a former law enforcement agent in Los Angeles who had extensive ties to the L.A. Mafia, founded another mob-backed casino that he named the "Golden Nugget." The Nugget, which billed itself as the largest casino in the country, earned a reputation with high rollers as a destination for no-limit poker games and blackjack hands. Needless to say, the gambling industry in that day and age was a mobster's game. During the Prohibition years, the majority of gangsters big and small pivoted their trade toward liquor smuggling and bootlegging, because that's where the real cash was. After alcohol became federally legal again in 1933, the Mafia lost their biggest cash cow, and all the former bootleggers went back to their old schemes.

One of the most promising of these old schemes was gambling. In 1931, the Nevada state government issued legislation that opened up the floodgates for legalized betting in a time when vices in America were being strictly regulated and scrutinized. Usually, the Mafia didn't operate within the realm of legal activities, but Nevada being the only place in America with almost zero gambling regulations meant that huge piles of cash were going to be flowing into the desert like never before. So, once illegal liquor production became obsolete, their next big score was already prepped for them, and America saw a new wave of bootleggers-turned-casino moguls. One of these men was Anthony Cornero, also known by his nickname "Tony the Hat." He was also known as "The Admiral," a moniker he earned from the several freighters he owned that he used to flood southern California with liquor that he smuggled down the coastline from Canada. Cornero's business was hard-hit when booze was made legal, but in the early 1930s he transitioned into a successful casino industrialist with the founding of The Meadows Hotel and Casino in Las Vegas Valley, one of the city's first ever major, licensed casino resorts.

The Meadows eventually ran into trouble as Cornero was feuding with the so-called Meyer and Bugs Gang, run by Bugsy Siegel and Meyer Lansky, two men who created the foundation for decades of mob domination of the Vegas casino industry. The pair were trailblazers—they even went so far as to convince Fulgencio Batista, the brutal Cuban dictator, to legalize gambling and allow them to open up casinos on the island. In Vegas, few could stand up to the likes of Bugsy and Lansky, who were both backed by some of the most powerful New York mobsters. But guys like Cornero continued to press on in Vegas in pursuit of their fortune. By the mid-1950s, Cornero was still in the city and was working on a brand-new venture. He was in the middle of opening the grand and famous Stardust Hotel. Before Cornero could open the casino in its full glory, he died under particularly suspicious circumstances. The Admiral had certainly left his mark on Las Vegas and the gambling world, but the man who eventually came to run the glamorous Stardust would completely redefine casino life and revolutionize the city of Las Vegas. That man was Frank "Lefty" Rosenthal.

To say that Lefty made an impression on Vegas would be an understatement. Frankly, the city had never seen anyone like him before. Plenty of guys connected to the mob passed through and some stayed for good, but none of them felt at home in that desert oasis as much as Lefty did. None of them were capable of calling shots like he was, and none of them had the same eye for consistency, optimization, or stats. Running a casino may seem like a sure-fire way to earn an easy profit, but in reality, it requires a keen sense of balance and management. The first real objective is to leave as little up to chance as possible. "Chance" and "luck" are meant to be nothing more than illusions designed to convince the gambler to believe he has an actual hope of winning. But like any other business, you can't simply bleed your customers dry. They are going to need money left over to continue coming back to the tables and try to win back their money. The rewards need to be enticing enough to keep them paying, while the odds need to be exact and precise to ensure that "the house" always gets paid. In the game of roulette, for example, for every one million dollars bet on the spins, a little north of $50,000 is expected to become pure profit for the house. The other $950,000 or so is returned to the gamblers through payouts, just enough to keep them believing that they can win it all back with a lucky spin.

Even if a player happened to hit a jackpot or win a big hand, they were almost guaranteed to lose it again if they continued to play. So, it was in the best interest of the casino to immerse the player as much as possible. Free drinks were a staple on casino floors because tipsy players were more likely to make reckless bets and lose track of time. Casino walls were completely bare of clocks, and the gaming floor had no windows so that players literally could not witness the passage of time. Even today, it's impossible to tell whether it's day or night from the inside of a casino floor. These were all the strategies, all the valuable bits of information that one needed to be successful in the Vegas' casino scene, and nobody understood them better than Lefty Rosenthal. Like many other Vegas pioneers, Lefty wondered to himself, what if he could beat the odds? What if he could outsmart the house? What if he could *become* the house? Meyer Lansky, one of the masterminds of early Vegas, thought the same way. But Lefty *lived* for the numbers, he *lived* for maximizing everything that could be maximized, and he understood the minds of gamblers better than anyone. He wanted to control the apparent randomness of gambling and harness it into millions of dollars' worth of profit. Lansky's own words perfectly describe how Lefty approached not only the betting world, but his entire life: "There's no such thing as a lucky gambler, there are just winners and losers. The winners are those *who control the game...* all the rest are suckers," (quoted in Gray, 2021).

So we know that a man like Lefty was destined to make it big in a place like Vegas, but the question still remains as to how exactly the city was transformed from a safe, idyllic tourist spot where gangsters could operate freely to a violent and bloody nest for the mob's most brutal enforcers, in just a few shorts years. Lefty himself wasn't a particularly violent person, nor was he fond of all the tactics of his old mob friends in Chicago. Unfortunately for the city of Las Vegas though, Lefty wasn't the only man that the Outfit had out in the desert. Joining Lefty a few years after he arrived was a promising young Outfit enforcer named Anthony "Tony the Ant" Spilotro. Spilotro was the guy that protected Lefty in everything he did, acting as the muscle behind the brain. Like Rosenthal, Spilotro had very big plans for Las Vegas, but their methods were not at all the same. He was not there simply to get as much cash from gamblers' pockets as humanly possible. He was there to make Las Vegas his own. He was there to transform the open and free market city into a kingdom where everyone knew who was king. And unlike his partner, violence was Tony the Ant's bread and butter. For better or worse, this was the city that Lefty and Spilotro had created—a lucrative and glamorous wonderland, soaked with blood. The following chapters will explore the lives of these two legendary men and the brilliant, violent innovations that they brought to Sin City.

CHAPTER 1

CHICAGO KID

Playing the Ponies

On June 12 of 1929 on the West Side of Chicago, Frank Rosenthal was born. At the time, the United States had been experiencing nearly a decade of increasing prosperity. More Americans than ever were owning cars, purchasing their own houses, and starting families, like the Rosenthals. Soon after Frank was born though, things started to look very grim. Earlier in the year, signs of an impending recession had been seen that made Americans across the country clutch their purse strings. Just months after his birth, the wild growth of the booming American economy came to an abrupt end, and in October with the stock market crash, the entire economy collapsed. Instead of buying homes, Americans were now struggling to pay their mortgages. Businesses went bankrupt, people stopped paying their debts, and people simply abandoned their homes en masse, since they couldn't afford to pay for them anyway. Homelessness was on the rise, and many people lost their jobs as unemployment skyrocketed. At the peak of the crisis, roughly one quarter of all Americans were without a job, the highest rate of unemployment in the country's history.

This was the America that Frank's generation inherited. For 10 long years, the country suffered with inflation and poverty, but young Frank was already luckier than most. Unlike most other American kids, especially ones in big cities like Chicago, Frank was insulated from most of the devastation and uncertainty that the Great Depression brought. The Rosenthal family was mercifully well-off, wealthy enough to get through the Depression relatively unaffected. Frank's father worked as an agriculture produce wholesaler and was a successful one at that. For the entirety of the Depression, his family was able to support themselves on his income alone, and his mother never had to look for work to supplement his salary. While most others in Chicago's West Side spent their days patrolling the city looking for anyone who would offer them some work for the day, young Frank and his family were secure with their day-to-day activities.

Frank's father wasn't just skimming by, though. He had disposable income to spend on his hobbies, a luxury that hardly anyone could afford in the early 1930s. The place that he most enjoyed spending this cash was at the horse racing tracks. He was certainly a betting man, and he even owned several of his own horses that he trained and raced whenever he could to make even more money. Frank, too, participated in this pastime. Again, unlike most kids his age, Frank was lucky enough not to have to toil away helping his family to scrape by. Instead, he spent most of his free time with his father down at the racetrack. He enjoyed being around the horses, and he always watched the races while he was there, but more importantly, he watched the bets. Horse racing is one of the oldest forms of gambling that is still around today, and it remains an incredibly popular hobby for rich and poor alike. King Charles II of England was notoriously fond of horse racing, earning it the nickname "the sport of kings." Of course, the reality of horse racing wasn't always as glamorous as this nickname might suggest, but Frank was nevertheless taken by it. He loved the sport, and he was fascinated not just by how many other people loved it, but by how much they were willing to spend betting on the outcome.

Needless to say, Frank was exposed to gambling at a very young age. He might not have understood yet exactly what drove people to make larger and larger bets even when they continued to make the wrong calls, but he nevertheless watched what they did like a hawk. Frank was never very social as a child, and often had difficulty making new friends. Numbers, however, came easy to him. In fact, they became almost an obsession for Frank in his pre-teen years. He was intrigued and fascinated by the concept of "odds" in the gambling world. With a watchful eye, he took careful note of the habits of the various gamblers that passed through the racetrack, including how much they bet, what odds attracted the most betters, and whether or not they would double down the next time after a substantial loss. He also took note of the payout ratios—why on earth would someone bet a hundred bucks on a horse that the experts decided had almost no chance of winning? On the other hand, why bother betting on a horse that would pay out pennies on the dollar? These questions consumed Frank in those days while he was at his father's side (and occasionally wandering off), and he spent a good portion of his childhood figuring out the answers for himself.

So, there was young Frank, against the brutal backdrop of the Great Depression, studying the mechanics of horseracing, honing his knowledge of the game, and analyzing the trends of the winning horses. This strange little habit continued well into his teenage years, but he became even more obsessive. He started compiling huge amounts of data and statistics on both horseracing and sports games like baseball. He organized it all into large files and folders that he kept in his room, categorizing and studying them as much as possible. Even when he had school in the morning, he would stay up until all hours of the night analyzing the historical stats and long-term winning trends, winning ratios, recent performances of horse jockeys and baseball pitchers, et cetera. Data on local races and ball games were the easiest to come by, especially in the pre-internet age of the 1930s and 1940s, but he compiled information on games and players all over the nation. Franks' goal here was obvious. He wasn't just a fan of numbers, and he didn't collect this data for the fun of it. If he had as much information as possible, he thought, perhaps he could eliminate the element of "chance" and actually predict the outcomes of races or games. He didn't want to be like the other clowns at the track who blew all their cash on an impulsive bet. He wanted to win. There's an old saying, particularly in the gambling world, that there is a sucker born every minute. But there, in Frank Rosenthal's bedroom late at night, behind a stack of folders and a dense sea of data, a winner was born; one who refused to be suckered by the odds.

A Born Gambler

By the time Frank had grown into a young man, he had already acquired the gambling itch. This was no surprise—he had spent the better part of his childhood studying the games, the bets, and the outcomes, and he put his knowledge to the test just as early as he could. While he was still in school, he was already a betting man. Whatever extra cash he could earn was used to make bets at the track first thing after school. Sometimes he didn't even wait until after school. If there was a particularly attractive game or a jockey with a hot streak, he would simply skip class to go make some bets. His truancy became more and more frequent as Frank got older, to the point that it started to seriously affect his education. Teachers wondered where he was always disappearing to, and his father would have likely been quite upset with young Frank if they didn't run into each other so often at the track while his father was skipping work. For the first time, Frank was finding out whether or not it was truly possible to beat the system. A lot of the time, it worked, and young Frank started to earn some serious cash, much more than any kid his age should have had.

Although Frank didn't have a lot of friends at this age, he wanted to share his talent for numbers with the ones that he did have. On more than one occasion, he convinced some of his buddies to ditch school with him and head down to the track to watch him make his prophetic wagers. Knowing little about the sport or the world of gambling, Frank's friends were amazed at his uncanny ability to predict winning horses. As he said himself, "my pals thought I was the Messiah," (Pileggi, 1995). But Frank was certainly no Messiah, and just like even the best gamblers in the world, young Frank did not always make the right call. In fact, he was quite well acquainted with the feeling of losing every penny that he had just earned. He had his good days, but as he said, "the next day I cut school again and went back to the track and lost it all," (Pileggi, 1995). Despite these inevitable losses, Frank was undeterred. His love for the races only got stronger, as did his love for profiting off of them. He continued to refine his strategy and learn plenty of valuable lessons about what it means to be a gambler.

After Frank acquainted himself with horse racing, he got more involved in the professional sports scene. He had a love for most sports and was an active better in most of them, including the National Football League (NFL) and college basketball. Without a doubt though, baseball was where his heart was. Given the type of person Frank was, this wasn't at all a surprise. All sports involve statistics of some sort, but baseball is particularly dense in statistics, and there is a myriad of metrics used to analyze the performance of both the player individually and the team as a whole. Plus, compared to most other sports, there is relatively little group interaction in baseball, which means that individual performance has a much more significant impact on the outcome of a given game. This also means that gathering data on baseball players for the purposes of gambling is both more intricate, time-consuming, and more valuable.

Having developed a strong interest in America's favorite pastime, young Frank would often hang around baseball diamonds around the city and in the bleachers of Chicago's famous Wrigley Field, the home of the Chicago Cubs since 1916. Here he would watch the games and compile whatever information he could, trying to gain an edge over the bookies who made the odds. But Frank wasn't the only one. At Wrigley Field he met a larger group of older gamblers who also liked to hang around the bleachers watching the games and trying to get rich. This particular group also enjoyed betting on college and professional basketball, but baseball was their bread and butter. Finally, Frank was no longer an outsider. He had met a group of like-minded people who were into the same kinds of things as him, and the older gamblers recognized this, accepting Frank as an up-and-comer, and as one of their own. Frank now had a small community among whom he could hone his craft, and there in the bleachers he learned some of the most valuable lessons on gambling in his life.

First, he learned not just how to reliably predict betting outcomes, but he learned to understand the mentality of his fellow gamblers. He observed first-hand what their vulnerabilities were and how they were taken advantage of in moments of inspiration or desperation. As an extension of this, he also learned all about the psychological tools and tricks that the bookies, or "the house," used to entice gamblers and get them to spend more cash. This intrigued Frank most of all. The bookies were the ones making the odds, dictating the flow of the bets, and raking in all the hard-earned income from the suckers, and best of all, their strategies were based on the same kind of data collection and analysis that Frank was so gifted at. Frank spent a lot of time observing one of the older bookies named Stacy, who became almost like an early mentor figure to the adolescent Frank. He was fascinated at the fact that guys would take *his* bets that he made with *his* odds, and he was enthralled at how Stacy was able to convince the degenerates he hung around with to keep coming back for more when they lost.

Frank also learned the intricacies of how guys like Stacy or Hymie (another senior gambler who was known as "Ace" by his friends) used their statistics to determine their odds, and how they discovered certain things that gave them an "edge" against everyone else. This was usually a key piece of information that few others knew about. One day, for example, after Frank and the other gamblers had their picks in and their bets all set for the Northwestern vs. Michigan State game, Hymie revealed to Frank a simple piece of little-known information that completely changed his calculations. Aside from knowing almost every detail worth knowing about the other players, he also happened to know that a particularly talented young black player named Johnny Green was recently made eligible to play after not appearing in a game all season. He was under the radar, and without him, Michigan State was the likely loser. But his season debut changed everything, and lo and behold, Michigan State upset Northwestern, and tons of folks lost their money. Frank very nearly lost his bet too, but he was luckily able to change his bet just in time with Hymie's latest tip. It was a close call, and Frank vowed to never be so careless with his bets again.

It was a wake-up call for young Frank. He didn't like that Hymie knew more than him, and he didn't like being on the outside looking in. From then on, *he* was going to be the guy with the inside info:

"I learned a hell of a lesson. I found out I wasn't as smart as I thought I was. I had depended upon people for too much. I had given them the power to make up my mind for me. I realized that if I wanted to spend my life gambling, pitting myself against the best bookmakers, there was no such thing as listening to people. If I was going to make a living doing this, I was going to have to figure it out for myself and do it all myself" (quoted in Pileggi, 1995).

So, Frank now had the tools to be able to make certain wagers enticing to betters while also ensuring that in the end, he would be the winner. This led to another important realization. Despite the perception that almost all gamblers had, there did not necessarily have to be such a thing as "luck" or "chance" in the betting world. There were plenty of methods to reduce the randomness of wagers or to eliminate the influence of chance altogether. Most of these methods, of course, were a little dishonest at best, or completely underhanded at worst. As we've seen in the introduction, cheating has been rampant in the sports world since the earliest years of human society, and gambling has always been one of the main drivers for it. In his childhood in Chicago, Frank had witnessed this crooked sportsmanship firsthand. He knew there were plenty of baseball pitchers who would intentionally walk the hitters, allowing the opposing team to load their bases. He knew there were hitters, on the other hand, who would strike out on purpose, missing easy pitches right down the middle. There were corrupt umpires who were easily paid off to make the wrong calls. In fact, there were entire teams willing to play terribly in important games for a payoff from the bookies who bribed them.

While most young sports fans would be hopelessly disillusioned to discover that there was so much corruption in their favorite pastime or that the players that they idolized had such little integrity, for Frank, this was a golden opportunity. With some convincing words and some well-placed dollars in the right pockets, perhaps the outcome of any game could be determined well before the game even started, and none of the betters would be the wiser. It was a great opportunity for the players as well, particularly in college sports where the players generally weren't paid for all their hard work and the prospect of entering the pro leagues was incredibly slim. So, why not make some money? They knew there were plenty of bookies eager to tip the scales in their favor, and if they couldn't make money by playing well, they could definitely make a bundle by playing poorly. This was true in basketball as well as baseball. Frank personally knew players who would spend hours practicing and perfecting their "missed shots." Of course, it didn't take a lot of skill to miss the basket, but by the mid-twentieth century, sports officials were hyperaware of the possibility of players rigging games. As we've seen in the introduction, there had already been major sports betting scandals that resulted in lifetime bans, so they had to be careful not to arouse too much suspicion. These "missed shots" couldn't look purposeful, they had to look like they were genuinely trying to score. Mastering rim shots and bad rebounds off the backboard turned into something of an art form, one that required as much practice and dedication as actual shots did, and it was all because of the influence and greed of the gambling world.

While still a young man in Chicago's West Side, hanging around with all the wrong people, Frank became a budding expert on gambling. He understood the games and how they were played. He understood how teams won and how teams lost, and he understood why people had an urge to bet their money. Most importantly, because of some important lessons in these early years of his life, he understood that in the gambling world, the ideas of "luck" and "chance" were simple illusions. Frank carried these lessons with him through his entire life, and it would only be a matter of time for this data-obsessed young Jewish man from Chicago to take the sports betting and gambling worlds by storm.

After becoming acquainted with the likes of Stacy and Hymie "Ace," Frank began his mission to perfect his understanding of the odds and to master his ability to manipulate them as best he could. In pursuit of the profits, he began studying even harder. He would spend hours on end listening to broadcasts of games from out of town and all across the United States. That wasn't enough though— any old schmuck could get a radio and listen to whatever game they wanted. Frank needed the info that not just anyone could get. He started purchasing subscriptions to local newspapers from towns near and far, ones you couldn't usually find in Chicago. These local papers often had little tidbits of information, small news pieces that the large national networks often thought were irrelevant. But in the betting world, no news was irrelevant. Perhaps, for example, Oklahoma State was favored in a matchup just before the playoffs. But what if their star forward rolled his ankle or twisted his knee at a recent practice? What if their lead defender got busted for a DUI two nights before the big game, and his eligibility was questionable? Or what if there were rumors of him taking up cocaine as a new hobby? These are the kinds of things that the local sports papers specialized in, but the national ones often had no space for. Armed with this knowledge, Frank was sure to have an invaluable edge on his bets.

Still, Frank wasn't always ahead of the curve even with dozens of local papers at his disposal. There were only a few newsstands in the city that stocked subscriptions to these kinds of niche papers, and while making his runs to pick them up, he inevitably ran into several groups of other guys who frequented the same stands. They were buying the same obscure local papers as Frank, and they were up to the exact same scheme. These guys were gambling pros, and they recognized Frank as a budding fellow betting man. Frank had found yet another group of like-minded individuals that accepted him into their circle, and he was able to hone his odds-making skills even further. Still, this meant that there were folks out there who had the same or better access to info than he did. So, he went a step further. Even in the local papers, Frank thought, there must still be potentially vital pieces of news that the editors deemed unworthy of publishing. So, he started making house calls. He somehow managed to get the names and phone numbers of reporters in various cities who reported on college games, and he would call them up with fake stories, fake voices, trying to extract whatever he possibly could out of them. Obviously, he couldn't do this for every one of the several dozens of games taking place every day across the country, so he started focusing on just a few. This way, while the bookies were trying to cover everything, Frank was specializing in a select group of games and he was almost certain to have more information than the guys making the bets.

It soon got to the point where Frank wasn't comfortable betting unless he knew for certain that the odds were in his favor. After all, he really hated losing, and he hated being suckered even more. If there were any variables that Frank believed he had left unaccounted for, he simply wouldn't bet at all. If there were a string of games where the odds were too close for comfort, he might not bet for weeks. But in that time, he had spare, Frank wasn't just waiting around. He was studying, analyzing, and sleuthing, always on the lookout for the next perfect game that would give him the perfect advantage. This is what set Frank apart from the other gamblers. The degenerates that he sometimes hung around with didn't wait for their moment. They bet on whatever they could, as often as they could, and they would wager as much as they could possibly afford. It didn't matter if it was a sure thing or a long shot, and it certainly wasn't a calculated art form like it was for Frank. His addiction wasn't gambling, it was winning.

Before long, Frank moved on from being just a player. He still made bets when he thought that the stars were aligned for a certain game, but now, as a young adult, he was ready for the next level. He didn't want to just try to beat the odds anymore. He wanted to make his own. He started up his own bookmaking service and began putting his odds-making skills, which he had been honing since childhood, to the real test. He was now perfecting his ability to fix the odds in his favor while also making them irresistible to the gamblers he had come to understand so well. And it worked. It took barely any time at all for Frank to become one of the best-known and successful bookies in Chicago's West Side, and he also earned a reputation as a legendary handicapper (basically, a person skilled at finding a certain "edge" in a given sports game). He was active in nearly every avenue of the sports betting world, and he always knew how to make the most cash. Every horse race, every baseball game, every basketball championship, Frank was there, analyzing and studying as much as he could, ready to make bank off of his marks. He clearly had a gift for making money, and in a place like the West Side, being able to make money made you very valuable, but not necessarily to the right people. As we'll see, some of Chicago's most violent and notorious gangsters took a strong interest in his abilities, and his handicapping got him in close with some very rough folks. As Frank himself said, "Every pitch. Every swing. Everything had a price" (quoted in Pileggi, 1995).

CHAPTER 2

THE FIX IS IN

By the time Frank was born in 1929, the connection between gambling and organized crime had already been a staple of Chicago's history for several decades. As far back as the 1860s, Chicago was rife with illegal gambling, and the whole industry was controlled by a notoriously corrupt businessman named Michael Cassius McDonald. His gambling ring was one of the first organized crime syndicates in the city, and he ushered in a new age of corruption for the city. Politicians and police officers alike were bought and paid for by McDonald's organization, and the man held near-immunity from the law. Later, in the early years of the 1900s, a new criminal powerhouse came to dominate the city's gambling underworld—the Chicago Outfit. Based in the city's South Side, the Outfit came to national prominence under the leadership of two of Chicago's most notorious crime lords: the southern Italian immigrant John Torrio, and the American-born Alphonse "Al" Capone, also known as "Scarface." Under Capone's leadership, the Outfit grew to become one of the most successful, prominent, and feared Mafia families in the entire USA, rivalling any of the Five Families of New York City. Through the era of Prohibition all the way up to the twenty-first century, the Chicago Outfit ran the city's criminal enterprises, and gambling and bookmaking were always some of their most reliable schemes. If you were an odds guy in Chicago and you were even remotely talented or successful, chances are you were affiliated in some way or another to the Outfit. Frank Rosenthal was definitely no exception.

The Chicago Outfit

Frank Rosenthal had been involved with members of the Chicago Mafia since shockingly early in his life. It would have been difficult for him not to be. Growing up on the West Side in a predominantly Sicilian or Italian neighborhood meant that you would invariably have known young men who went on to join the Outfit. Even being Jewish, Frank grew up with plenty of Outfit guys, and was close friends with several of them. As we'll see, one of these childhood friends was a violent young man named Tony Spilotro, and the two of them together would go on to make history. Before that though, their relationship was much simpler. Frank was the guy with an uncanny knack for fixing odds, and the Outfit guys protected him and gave him avenues for earning. The Mafia had traditionally associated only with fellow Italians (sometimes they had to be full-blooded Sicilian), but in reality, these "morals" were compromised when big money was involved. If you were capable of making money, then it didn't matter who you were or what your background was, the Outfit wanted a piece of your action.

When Frank was a late-teenager, he began working for a Chicago-based sports betting service run by Donald Angelini and Bill Kaplan, commonly referred to as "Angel-Kaplan." These two guys ran arguably the largest betting operation in the entire Chicago metropolitan area (the Outfit's gambling ventures also included things like illegal casinos and high-stakes card games). And unsurprisingly, it was under the protection and supervision of the Outfit. In fact, Angelini himself was a "made man" in the Family, meaning that he was an official member deemed "untouchable" by anyone outside the Family without official endorsement. He was an important guy to work for, especially when it came to gambling. Angelini was eventually made a *caporegime* in the Outfit, which was a high rank that commanded respect. He had his own crew operating out in Elmhurst, a small Chicago suburb about 18 miles from the city center that was home to a massive ring of gambling rackets run by Angelini. Like Frank, he was gifted with numbers and understood the minds of gamblers. His knack for this particular trade had earned him the moniker "the Wizard of Odds," and whether you were making or taking bets in Chicago, chances are you were indirectly doing business with this man.

Being one of the top guys in charge of the Outfit's gambling sector was no minor status to hold. The West Side's own Tony "Big Tuna" Accardo, who had become acting boss of the entire Outfit by the late 1940s, used to be the big man in charge of Chicago's gambling before he inherited the entire throne. Needless to say, Angelini was in a powerful and privileged position, and being able to work for him at the young age of 19 was like a dream come true for Frank. While working for Angelini and Kaplan, Frank made a lot of important connections that would come in handy later in his life, and he earned a reputation as a reliable earner with some of the top Outfit guys. Some of the bosses had known Frank since he was a little kid, so he didn't have much to worry about in terms of competition. Still, there were other odds makers working for the Outfit, so Frank had to sharpen his tactics even more. He knew the other guys' strategies and he made sure he was always a step ahead. He was still spending hours incessantly calling (and borderline harassing) local sports reporters in towns with teams that Frank had added to his shortlist of gambling targets, lying and conniving to uncover anything relevant that never made it to print. For the games that Frank decided to focus on, he was often one of only a handful of people in the entire nation that had the "full story." The detail of the information he gathered in these little investigations could have rivalled that of any private investigator in the city. Because Frank wasn't Italian, he could never become an official member of the Chicago Mafia, but despite this, he was quickly becoming one of their most valuable assets.

It didn't take long for just about every bookmaker in the city to learn Frank Rosenthal's name. He was simply that good of a handicapper. It got to the point that other bookies would actually change their own odds and payouts depending on what odds Frank was giving because his success rate was so high. Of course, he still made his fair share of mistakes and lost out on more than a couple of big games, but his predictions were about as close as you could come to a sure thing in the world of sports betting. Pretty soon, Frank would discover that his reputation was actually growing far beyond the city limits of Chicago. For now, though, he was still just a Chicago kid, trying to perfect his craft alongside and under the protection of some of the most ruthless gangsters in America.

Around the same time Frank started working for Angel-Kaplan, he also started hanging out at a local cigar shop owned by two guys that he knew only as George and Sam. As it turns out, the two business partners were connected to both the New York City and

Chicago Mafias. The pair were originally from New York but were given the blessing of the Outfit to open up shop in Chicago. Their cigar parlor was a popular spot for all kinds of Illinois wise guys, but it wasn't just because they enjoyed the products. It was because in a secret room in the back of the shop, George and Sam ran a large sports betting racket and also hosted many illegal card games for high rollers. Frank wasn't directly involved but he did benefit from the knowledge of some senior mob gamblers. More importantly, he learned a lesson about how easy it was to corrupt the morals of the people who were supposed to be enforcing gambling laws. Since the early days of organized crime in Chicago, even before the legendary Prohibition era of Al Capone, the Chicago Police Department was notoriously corrupt, and they remained so well into the later decades of the twentieth century. George and Sam took advantage of this. To Frank's surprise, their backroom gambling operation was not exactly a well-kept secret. It had operated for years with the full knowledge of the Chicago Police, and they had received their blessing to operate in the city so long as the cops got their cut. Greasing the right palms was a very valuable tool for being able to operate in peace, as Frank quickly learned.

Frank was never really involved much in the violent aspects of the Outfit's criminal operations. Most of the "numbers" guys rarely were. Still, having grown up around connected guys for his entire childhood and adolescence, mob life was like second nature to him. In this kind of environment, it was very hard for Frank to stay "straight." He could have been an upstanding citizen and used his skills to make some money for himself on the side, but instead, everything Frank did was helping enrich Chicago mobsters, whom he had inextricable connections with. This, as it turns out, was a dangerous trend that ended up haunting him later in his life. Frank would always be tipping off his friends in the Outfit as to what his handicaps were and what odds he had calculated, and he would always let them know what games the hot bets were at. To him, of course, it was more like he was just helping out his pals, not some random, violent gangsters. Outside of this work with Angelini and Kaplan, the information and tips that he funneled to gambling wise guys made him very popular, especially among the Outfit bosses. Every day, he was becoming a more and more valuable tool. Around this time, Frank also earned himself an affectionate nickname. Giving nicknames has for decades been a time-honored tradition in the Italian-American Mafia, and Frank came to be known as "Lefty" by all of his connected pals. There are a few conflicting stories for how Lefty earned this moniker, but it appears likely that it was a simple reference to the fact that he happened to be left-handed.

By the time the 1950s rolled around, Frank "Lefty" Rosenthal was in his early twenties. At this young age, he had already developed a close personal relationship with Fiore Buccieri, the notorious and feared Outfit boss who was in charge of all of their operations on the city's West Side. The two had known each other for a long time, and because of his privileged position, Lefty was able to get much closer to Buccieri, who was also known as "Fifi," than even most of the highest-ranking Outfit guys. Lefty and Fifi could often be seen around Chicago, driving around together and talking, presumably about their shared interest in the gambling rackets. This was likely a source of resentment for quite a few guys in the Family who would have protested the idea of an outsider getting closer to the boss than they could ever hope to be. Luckily, Lefty was just too valuable to be touched. At least for now.

Despite the jealousy aimed in Lefty's direction, Fifi was a very big deal in Chicago and just being seen with him was huge for Lefty's reputation. Born in 1907, Buccieri was a notorious loan shark around Chicago and had been one for quite some time. He was a long-time gangster whose rap sheet dated all the way back to the mid-1920s, by which time he had already earned a reputation as a ruthless gangster. He made his bones working as a "button man" (a kind of codeword for a mob assassin) for the legendary bootlegger and Outfit boss Al Capone, which alone made Fifi a man worthy of respect in the criminal underworld. During American Prohibition, which lasted for 13 years between 1920 and 1933, there were violent gang wars that were waged over control of local bootlegging markets in major cities all across the United States. The violence was particularly bloody in Chicago, the home territory of Capone and his thugs. The most famous of these occurred between the Outfit, the predominantly Irish gang run by Bugs Moran, and Joseph Saltis' crew. Buccieri was a veteran of these so-called "beer wars," and unlike Moran or Saltis, he was on the winning side. This made the West Side boss something of a legend among Chicago's younger mafiosi.

Of course, it wasn't just his proximity to Al Capone that put Fifi in the position he was in. He had earned himself quite a fearful reputation on his own as well, one which he kept up well into the 1950s. In fact, it only seemed to have gotten worse as time went on—in the early 1960s, amid a string of arrests made against the Outfit, Buccieri was rumored and widely believed to have kidnapped a suspected rat and tortured him to death. The torture reportedly lasted three whole days before the victim finally died of his injuries. It should go without saying that Fifi was a man that

Lefty and everybody else in the Outfit wanted to impress and keep happy. Out of all of them though, few were as capable of earning Fifi reliable income as Lefty. He had mastered the scheme of gambling and with all the connections he had made, he had become indispensable: "Lefty was in a position to hear about doped horses, fixed fights, crooked refs, and just about every gambling scam you could dream up, and he always knew just the right people to share that information with," (Pileggi, 1995).

Because of all this, Lefty had almost unmatched access to and influence over the West Side boss. This was a very good position to be in, and it paid off when it came to helping save the life of a friend of his, someone who is very important to our story here: Anthony "Tony the Ant" Spilotro. Once, Buccieri's wife was robbed at gunpoint at their home while Fifi was away, and the armed intruder made off with a small fortune in cash and jewelry. When news of this got around, nobody knew how Fifi would react and the entire West Side and beyond were in fear of what he might do in retaliation. They were right to be afraid, because the enraged Fifi quickly organized and conducted a city-wide investigation into the robbery. He had his men with their eyes and ears to the streets everywhere, trying to uncover anything about who did it or who gave the order. Despite the fear that the boss injected into the city, it potentially provided a golden opportunity to any opportunistic gangster to get in Buccieri's good graces. Many began to fear that they would be thrown under the bus as a suspect just to win his approval, or to get his suspicions off themselves. Times like these are when the inherent selfishness, greed, and pride of the Mafia can be the difference between life and death.

A few weeks after the robbery, some unknown wise guy decided that the reign of terror needed to end. To do that, he needed a name. There was only one guy in all of Chicago that just about everyone would believe had the balls to organize a robbery of someone like Buccieri, and that guy was Tony Spilotro. The rat told Buccieri as much, and it immediately made sense to the boss. Buccieri, who was a much higher rank in the Outfit than Spilotro, who was just a soldier at the time, called for an immediate "meeting" with Spilotro at Buccieri's home. Given the situation in Chicago at the time, Spilotro knew exactly what the meeting was and what was going to happen to him when he arrived. He also knew that his long-time pal Lefty Rosenthal was very close with the chief and was one of the few people whose counsel Buccieri might actually listen to. Spilotro pleaded with Lefty for him to attend the "meeting" with the chief alongside him, and Lefty reluctantly agreed. At the risk of enraging Buccieri further, Lefty arrived at his house with Spilotro, and although Fifi intended on interrogating the young soldier, it was very clear that there was a planned assassination that night. Even knowing that the boss wanted him dead, and that Fifi was notoriously violent, the aggressive Spilotro couldn't keep his mouth shut. He was uncooperative and sarcastic, and Fifi nearly strangled him to death after he made a snide remark when accused of being behind the robbery. It was only due to Lefty's pleas that Buccieri released his grip on Spilotro's throat. Lefty reassured Fifi that there was no actual evidence that pointed to Tony, only conjecture and hearsay from another gangster who may have had a vendetta against Tony or simply wanted to throw Fifi off his trail. Moreover, Lefty reminded Fifi how close he and Tony were, and that Lefty would never be there defending Tony if he knew he was behind the robbery. In the end, cooler heads prevailed and Buccieri allowed Tony to live, but he was on thin ice. Tony now owed his life to Lefty, and their bond grew even stronger.

After the Buccieri robbery fiasco, Lefty had proven himself to be indispensable to more than one of his Outfit cronies in Chicago. Still, his reputation was reaching far beyond Illinois. After just a few years of working with Angelini and Kaplan, Lefty received a very special invitation from a very important man (at least in the gambling scene). His name was Gil Beckley, and that was a name Lefty knew very well. Beckley was, at the time, easily the number one bookmaker in the entire United States and he maintained that title for years, outlasting countless national competitors. To put it simply, his operation was massive. Although in later years advancements in law enforcement tactics reduced Beckley to operating out of payphone booths on the street, he was the gambling kingpin in the late 1940s and early 1950s. As it turned out, Beckley was hosting a special guests-only event night for a local boxing match, and he had rented some luxurious spaces for his most favored guests. One of those men was Lefty. According to Lefty himself, he and Beckley had actually been quite friendly with each other for some time. They had spoken to each other on the phone several times over the previous year or so, but the two had never actually met in person. The fact that someone like Gil Beckley, a bona fide magnate in Lefty's world, not only liked him and wanted to meet him but thought of him as one of the few people to invite to his special event, was monumental for the young oddsmaker. Perhaps even more than his relationship with Buccieri, being on Beckley's radar was huge for his reputation.

Although Beckley's business ethics and philosophy were a bit shadowy by most people's standards, he was still a world apart from the normal crowd that Lefty hung around with. Lefty had known gangsters his whole life and had been a mobbed-up Outfit associate since the first time he started feeding gambling tips to his wise guy pals. Beckley was different. He was not necessarily a stranger to violence and had been implicated in some unsavory acts during his national feud with one of his main bookmaking competitors, Red Dodson, but he certainly wasn't the type to get involved with people like Buccieri. He wasn't a gangster and he tried to distance himself from them whenever possible. According to him, this was apparently his secret to his longevity and success. When he met Lefty at his fight night event, he immediately liked him, but he had some stern advice for the young fixer, who Beckley already knew had some shady connections. The advice was basically a warning. First, if Lefty wanted to avoid trouble, he needed to distance himself from the guys in the Outfit. Beckley had been around long enough to know that in the Mafia, loyalty was only worth as much as the money you earned them last week. Second, he told Lefty to stay out of the limelight as much as possible. Guys in their field didn't need to be household names to be successful, and unwanted notoriety inevitably meant attention from law enforcement. It was wise advice that Lefty should have heeded, but as we'll see later in his career, he took exactly none of it to heart.

Tony the Ant

The night that Lefty convinced Fiore Buccieri to spare the life of Spilotro was only the beginning of the pair's long and troubled history together. Over the years, their paths intersected more and more, and understanding their relationship is vital both in understanding the fate of the two men, and the fate of the city that they eventually took by storm. But first, we have to understand the kind of man Tony was in the first place, because he and Frank Rosenthal were, surprisingly, completely unalike. Born in May of 1938, Anthony Spilotro was nearly 10 years younger than Lefty, but that didn't stop the two of them from bonding. Born to Italian immigrants in Chicago, he grew up just a few streets over from Lefty in the West Side, in a small wood-frame home. Despite living so close to one another, Lefty and Tony did not have the same upbringing. Unlike the Rosenthals, the Spilotro family was large and impoverished, which was more or less typical for Italian immigrant communities. Tony was forced to share a single room with all five of his brothers. In this environment, it's no surprise that Tony dreamed of a life where he could have it all.

While there were differences in Lefty and Tony's situations in childhood, they did share at least one thing in common. Tony, as well as all of his brothers, were also exposed to the Mafia lifestyle from a very early age. Being Italian, the Mafia presence in their neighborhood was felt even more strongly. Tony's father, Pasquale "Patsy" Spilotro, was believed to have mob connections to the Outfit, and the restaurant he owned on Grand Avenue was known to be a popular hangout for Outfit soldiers and capos. It was also a popular spot to make backroom dealings, many of which the Spilotro brothers witnessed firsthand while helping out at the restaurant. This was the environment Tony grew up in, and like Lefty, it didn't take much convincing for him to get more involved as he grew older.

Growing up alongside Tony and his brothers was another young man named Frank Cullotta, who was just a few months younger than Tony. Although the pair later became famous for their partnership, their friendship did not have the most auspicious start. As kids, both Tony and Frank ran small shoe-shine businesses on the street. Much of their clientele were Outfit guys, and before long, the two began competing for their business. Both claimed their home neighborhood as their own turf, and hilariously, the competition grew quite fierce out on the street as they each tried to claim their own territory. Their little shoe shining turf war came to an abrupt end, however, and the two soon became inseparable allies. And it was all because of their fathers. Frank's father, Joe Cullotta, was also a gangster of some notoriety in Chicago, and as it happened, he was one of Patsy Spilotro's frequent customers at the restaurant. Joe, like most of the other wise guys, liked Patsy and respected his business. In turn, the senior Spilotro was happy to serve him and his friends, despite their questionable reputation. But some years earlier, before Tony and Frank ever met, Patsy was having some trouble. At the time, gangs of Sicilian-born mobsters familiarly known as "the Black Hand" were harassing Patsy, shaking him down for protection money. In the old country, particularly in Sicily, it was common for Mafiosi to extort business owners, both big and small, for cash payments. This was for the benefit of simply being allowed to stay open and operate in the gangsters' neighborhood. Many Mafiosi who immigrated to the United States and Canada took this habit along with them to their new homes, and they typically targeted the close-knit Italian migrant communities, whose members would already be accustomed to the practice of essentially paying tribute to the local chief.

Fearing for his life and the survival of his business, Tony's father looked for a way to avoid paying the Black Hand while also securing his family's safety and livelihood. Patsy turned to one of the few people who he knew could help: Joe Cullotta. Joe certainly didn't like the idea of his pal, a restaurant owner in his own neighborhood, being extorted and threatened by rival gangsters. So, as the story goes, Joe got together several of his associates, and together they confronted the Black Hand gangsters and killed them. It sent a clear message to everyone else that Patsy Spilotro and his restaurant were off-limits. After young Tony heard about this story, he decided it was time to bury the hatchet with Frank, who Tony may have considered himself indebted to. From this point forward, Tony and Frank were closer than ever, and they began a friendship that would follow them all the way from Chicago, Illinois to Las Vegas, Nevada.

Despite operating a mob hangout and being pals with someone like Joe Cullotta, it seems that Tony's father was never actually involved with the Mafia's illegal activities and certainly wasn't someone with a penchant for violence. This means that Tony's eventual rise to Mafia stardom was not necessarily a foregone conclusion in the late 1940s. But there is no question that Tony always had the attitude, the boldness, and the recklessness to make people fear him. Interestingly, both Tony and Frank were unusually short, which was noticeable since childhood. Since this made them likely targets of bullying, some speculate that this led the pair of them to try to become as vicious and as aggressive as possible, to deter anyone who might try to take advantage of them. This likely was something that they bonded over, as they both watched the other's back and protected each other in a neighborhood where being weak made you prey. They both wanted to be respected, not made fun of, and in many Italian immigrant communities in America's large cities like Chicago, there were few better ways to demand respect (and fear) than joining the Mafia.

So, the two young entrepreneurs had already set themselves on a path that led to violence and crime, but it was actually Tony's older brother Vic Spilotro that first introduced the two of them to Mafia life and "organized crime." Vic earned his money through one of Chicago's favorite criminal pastimes, operating a small bookmaking business in town that was backed up by the Outfit. Both Tony and Frank were fascinated and intrigued by Vic's gangster lifestyle. As Cullotta said of Vic, "I became convinced he was a gangster because of the way he dressed and that he always had a big wad of money with him," (Cullotta, 2017). Frank also noticed how much Tony looked up to him: "Tony idolized Vic and his lifestyle. Vic introduced Tony to a lot of his associates as he was growing up—more guys with nice clothes, women, and money," (Cullotta, 2017). Vic also ran some local illegal craps games, and sometimes, he would let Tony and Frank play. Vic's games certainly weren't for high rollers by any means, but this is where Tony first got a real taste for gambling. Even Frank took note of how natural and skillful Tony seemed as a gambling man. Like Lefty, Tony was now on a path that inevitably ended in one place: Las Vegas, the biggest casino town in the world.

Vic Spilotro was definitely one of the main factors in both Tony and Frank becoming more involved with organized crime as they got older. But it wasn't just the glamor and the cash that Vic showed them. He also introduced the pair to the power of violence, and how you can use it as a tool to get what you want. Vic wasn't a big-time gangster by any means, and to the higher-ups in the Chicago Outfit, he was a nobody. Still, he was a guy that commanded respect, at least from the people who were below him on the gangster totem pole. Vic wasn't afraid to throw his weight around when the situation called for it, and he would always use his reputation for violence to his advantage. One day at school, Vic showed them how they could solve all of their problems with a little bit of bloodshed.

As the story goes, both Tony and Frank attended the Moses Montefiore Academy in Chicago's Near West Side. The school was established in 1929 as a place to educate and rehabilitate young students who exhibited emotional disorders related to violence or other anti-social behavior. It's not known exactly what incident (or string of incidents) led to the pair of them being sent to Montefiore, but they were certainly troublemakers from a young age. Tony and Frank both quickly realized that the school was heavily racialized, and that they were two of only a handful of white students. There were even fewer Italian white students. As a result, they were often the victims of bullying and assault by the black students. It eventually got to the point that the pair were afraid to go to the school where they would be confronted by gangs of violent students who drastically outnumbered them. When Vic heard of their troubles at Montefiore, he decided to take matters into their own hands. He drove the two to school one day, armed with a loaded pistol. Apparently, the enraged Vic drove straight through the school's fence right around lunchtime, hopped out, and burst into the cafeteria where the other students were eating. Tony and Frank apparently pointed out to Vic the ringleader of the group of boys who had been giving them trouble. Vic then proceeded to kidnap the kid at gunpoint and escort him to his car. The four of them drove off with the boy then took him out and brutally assaulted him. Vic drove back to the school and dumped the boy there, bloody and bruised. Tony and Frank were both kicked out of Montefiore after the incident, and Frank was sent to another reformatory school. Despite this, the lesson they learned was clear: there was no problem that violence couldn't solve.

Frank and Tony, who later became known as "Tony the Ant," were a pair of kids prepped for a life in the Mafia. It wouldn't be very long before their stories intersected with that of Lefty Rosenthal's, and although Frank Cullotta is a more peripheral figure in the overall story of Lefty and Tony in Las Vegas, he is still important in understanding the kind of person Tony Spilotro was. The pair were already inseparable and while Tony was earning his reputation, Frank was always there in the background. In later years, Frank remembered Tony telling him exactly what his plans were, to climb to the very top of the Mafia underworld, right by Frank's side: "Frankie, I'm going to become one of them. Someday I'm going to be a boss, and I'll take you with me," (Cullotta, 2017). When these individuals finally made their way to Las Vegas in the Nevada desert, the city would be forever changed, and that was as much the fault of Tony and Frank as it was of Lefty.

CHAPTER 3

"THE BOOKIES GO TO FLORIDA AND THE PLAYERS EAT SNOWBALLS..."

Throughout the rest of the 1950s, Tony Spilotro became closer and closer to Lefty as well as Frank Cullotta. He was building a loyal and strong group of allies just as Lefty was gaining a national reputation as a renowned fixer and oddsmaker. When the 1960s came around though, it was a whole new era, and plenty of things changed, both for Lefty and Tony. Tony had long since graduated from his petty crimes like shoplifting and pickpocketing, and Lefty was in the process of expanding his bookie operation. In 1954, Tony's father, Pasquale, tragically died, and his mother, Antoinette, was left to raise her large family alone. This shifted a lot of responsibility onto Tony and his brothers, particularly Vic, one of the eldest. This reaffirmed for the Spilotro boys that they needed to do whatever they could to make money. After his father died, Tony dropped out of school altogether and spent basically all of his time committing crime. His first arrest came at 16 years old, for which he was given probation and a slap on the wrist, but as he got older, his crimes became more serious, and his arrests became more frequent. By 20 years old, he had already had numerous run-ins with the law. Lefty was more cautious. He wasn't a violent guy or a petty thug, so he wasn't piling up a rap sheet like Tony was. Still, there's no doubt about it: Lefty was a criminal. As the 1950s progressed, businesses like Lefty's were getting squeezed more and more, and before long, he was finding himself in big trouble in his native Chicago.

Trouble in the 1960s

When the new decade hit, things really began to change for Lefty and Tony both. Spilotro's enterprise had grown from petty crime and thievery and had now earned a reputation for himself as a renowned burglar. Judging from his earliest street crimes, it seems obvious that Tony always had a taste for stealing, and in his 20s, high-profile burglaries of expensive homes and businesses became his main play, and he had become quite skilled at it over the years. Of course, he tended to focus on cash and large items of value, but realistically, Tony would steal just about anything that wasn't bolted down or behind lock and key. Even if it was, he never had a problem with a little dirty work if he had to smash open some doors or break through some walls. His tactics were a bit too loud and messy for Lefty, but they got the job done. Tony eventually even put together his own team of elite burglars that he kept on standby for special or important jobs, each one specializing in alarm systems, lockpicking, safecracking, etc. Frank Cullotta, who grew up stealing right alongside Tony, was his right-hand man in their burgling operation, and he would graduate to armed robbery later in life.

In 1960, Tony married a girl he had been dating for a while named Nancy Stuart, who worked as a waitress at a local restaurant (she was one of the few women in his life who was shorter than he was). The two would remain married for Tony's entire life. Just a few years after Tony started his family life, he was developing his Mafia life. He started making important connections to Outfit guys like Vinnie Inserro, and Inserro introduced him to guys like Chuckie Nicoletti, who was a notorious Outfit hitman, and Joseph Lombardo, also known as "Joey the Clown," a high-ranking made guy and trusted advisor. In 1962, Tony joined up with Sam DeStefano's crew. DeStefano, who was also known as "Mad Sam," was known to be incredibly sadistic, and he was arguably one of the most mentally unstable criminals in the history of the Mafia, right up there with future Genovese Family boss Vincent "the Chin" Gigante. In 1963, a year after joining with DeStefano, Tony became a made guy.

By the time Tony was made, he had already earned his reputation for brutality, ruthlessness, and violence. While he was still just an associate in Mad Sam DeStefano's crew, he was given his first hit contract. It was an important one, too. Sometime earlier, the Outfit had learned the identity of two individuals who committed a pair of murders in Chicago's Elmwood Park. Elmwood is one of Chicago's historically Italian-American communities, and at the time, it was home to many high-up leaders of the Outfit and other criminal organizations. As a result of this, Elmwood Park had long been considered "untouchable." Crimes were not meant to take place there, and it was to be kept as pristine as possible, both for the peace of the bosses living there and for keeping away unwanted police attention. Needless to say, murder was not allowed to happen there under any circumstances, and in this case, it was grounds for a death sentence. As it turned out, the two killers responsible were a couple of young hustlers and burglars named Billy McCarthy and Jimmy Miraglia. The young partners had begun earning a reputation for themselves, but messing around where the Outfit bosses lived was their last mistake.

Tony was put in charge of the hits, but they weren't just hits. The bosses needed to send a clear message to all of Chicago's underworld that this could not happen again. So, when Tony and the hit crew he brought along with him eventually sniffed out and caught up to McCarthy, something worse than death was in store for him. Spilotro's men kidnapped McCarthy and proceeded to torture him in some of the most gruesome ways imaginable before finally ending his life. The torture was partly to demonstrate what would happen to those who violated the territory rules of the top Mafia echelon, and partly because Spilotro needed to know where to find Miraglia, who at the time of McCarthy's torture, was still at large. McCarthy was apparently unwilling to reveal his accomplice's whereabouts at first, but before long Tony was able to squeeze it out of him. Literally. Apparently, one of Tony's methods of torture was placing McCarthy's head in a large tool vise and tightening it until his skull nearly crushed completely. When McCarthy's corpse was eventually found, his eye had exploded out of its socket and his skull was damaged. Eventually the hit squad caught up to Miraglia too, and he was tortured and killed in a similar fashion. Both of them were put out of their misery with a knife across the throat, and their bodies were dumped together in the trunk of a car.

The double homicide, which the media took to calling the "M&M Murders" after their bodies were discovered, skyrocketed Tony's credibility and reputation within the Outfit, and the success of his first hit likely contributed to the leadership's decision to induct Spilotro formally into the legendary former Family of Al Capone.

By the mid-1960s, Tony was well-known, even famous in some circles, around Chicago. Lefty generally felt more comfortable behind the scenes and did most of his work out of the spotlight, but Tony hit that city with a bang. He was already a prime suspect in the McCarthy and Miraglia murders (the police also had a feeling that Mad Sam DeStefano was personally involved), and a string of more and more spectacular crimes in the West Side and beyond, in which Spilotro was also implicated, were drawing him a ton of attention from the law at such an early stage of his career. Tony apparently wasn't content to keep his criminal activity confined to Chicago though. The entire world, as far as he was concerned, was up for grabs. Tony acted on this belief in 1964 when he and an associate of his left Illinois with their wives on a long vacation through Europe. Secretly, however, Tony and the other gangster had planned a series of robberies and break-ins across nearly every country that they planned on visiting. The goal was obviously to gather as much loot as possible and return to the US to fence it off, but it didn't work out quite as planned. To the dismay of his wife Nancy, their dream vacation was repeatedly interrupted by Tony's arrests. He was kicked out of several countries and told not to return, and by the time the two couples reached France, the French police were already aware that they were on their way. When the Spilotros and their companions returned home, American officials seized them immediately and searched them, finding hidden diamonds and other gems on Tony's person. They also found jewelry and burglar's tools, all of which were seized. Supposedly, Tony managed to sneak out some diamonds hidden in Nancy's large hairdo.

As Tony's notoriety increased, so did his operations. He had his hand in a lot of things, whatever it took to be an earning member of the Outfit. Tony had a lot of associates working under him at this time, but he never liked mixing his crews. For all of the several scams Tony had running, from loansharking to gambling, he had a separate, dedicated crew with as little overlap as possible. Cullotta, being one of Tony's closest friends, was one of the few exceptions. Cullotta was involved in many of his schemes, but surprisingly, even he never got introduced to Lefty until quite a few years down the road. When they finally did meet though, it was a big deal for Cullotta to meet someone as well-connected as Lefty was. Lefty was already a few years older than Tony and Frank, but he was also someone who could talk back and give attitude to high-ranking Outfit guys with impunity, because he was just that valuable. Even Tony had to be careful what he said to Lefty when the two of them had disagreements. Lefty wasn't impenetrable though, and the crackdowns of the late 1950s would soon be taking their toll on the number one odds-fixer in Illinois.

In the late 1950s, criminals that ran illegal gambling rackets and schemes had long been considered among the worst of the worst when it came to vice crimes. This was the era after Prohibition ended, so bootlegging was no longer lucrative and thus no longer a source of public concern, and before the infamous era of the so-called "war on drugs," so peddlers of cocaine and heroin were not yet the number one public enemy. On a national level, mobsters and their gambling rackets didn't have much to fear for a long time because of FBI Director J. Edgar Hoover's lax attitude toward organized crime. On a local level, the Chicago Police Department wasn't much to fear either. Chicago cops had long been on the payroll of the Outfit, and some of the highest-ranking members of the force had essentially been in the pockets of gamblers like Lefty and his bosses. When the 1960s rolled around though, the Chicago gambling landscape was beginning to look very different. The federal government had begun their crackdown on organized crime, and the effects of this trickled down to the local level in Chicago, where police actually started targeting the goons running the sportsbooks and the illegal backroom card games. This included Lefty Rosenthal.

In the early years of the 1960s, Lefty was brought in on multiple charges of attempting and succeeding to rig sports games. The allegations stretched over multiple instances and included charges of bribing both players and referees. While Lefty was certainly guilty of helping to rig numerous games over the course of his career, he managed to avoid a jail sentence. It was Lefty's very first gambling arrest, which was probably the reason for the leniency, but most others weren't so lucky. The future of Chicago was looking grim, and Lefty saw it. Plus, even though he was still a free man, he had now become a publicly known figure. Worse, he was now an obvious target of the Chicago PD, and Lefty would have a much more difficult time operating with them breathing down his neck. The advice of Gil Beckley, to avoid unwanted attention at all costs, had been abandoned the moment Lefty decided to ride around in public with Fifi Buccieri, and now he was paying the price. The era of law enforcement being complicit in the city's gambling rings was now largely dead, and Chicago had now become a bit too dangerous for Lefty to continue his operation.

Moving to Miami

Powerful Mafia Families across the nation tended to stretch out their influence into other national markets. The Bonanno Family of New York City was known to have extensive operations in Arizona and parts of Canada. The Patriarca Family in New England claimed territory in both Providence, RI, and Boston, MA, and as far north as Maine. Some cities, like Miami, were host to numerous national syndicates that each controlled a portion of a certain criminal industry. By the 1960s, the Chicago Outfit already had a long history in Miami and were often allied with the Trafficante Family, who were native to the Tampa Bay area of Florida. Their domination of the city's underground gambling rackets dated back a little over a decade. In 1949, while the legendary Tony Accardo was just a few years into his reign as Chicago boss, Miami's gambling was controlled by a crime syndicate known simply as "S and G." At the time, the group was running an operation worth nearly $27 million (Chepesiuk, 2017). Then, Chicago moved in.

The Outfit had a lot of resources at their disposal, and when they started to challenge S and G for control, it was only a matter of time before they seized it. The Outfit, after all, had control over the Continental Press Service. Continental, which the anti-Mafia crusading Senator Estes Kefauver once labelled the country's number one public enemy, was the nation's leading source of almost instantaneous information on races from across the country. They supplied prompt and up-to-date decisions and last-minute alerts about weather conditions and the like. Using employees stationed at the numerous local tracks, they received their information by telephone, and it was then disseminated through the country using

Western Union lines. Continental was vital in elevating racetrack betting from a local event to a nationwide phenomenon, enabling betters from anywhere to make more reliable bets on races happening on the other side of the country. Needless to say, it was an incredibly valuable resource for bookies, and the Outfit knew it.

S and G used Continental Press Service regularly, but when the Outfit decided to seize control of the area's gambling market, it was a tool for Chicago to use against them. The Outfit cut off Continental service to S and G after the syndicate tried to resist. Later, Chicago disabled the wire service across the entire state of Florida, meaning that local bosses could not communicate nearly as easily or promptly with each other and with their bosses, nor could they get to-the-minute updates on races in other parts of the country. It was an aggressive move, but an effective one. Shortly after this point, S and G had very little choice but to accept Outfit takeover. Chicago essentially absorbed S and G's business and began dominating the gambling rackets in Miami and elsewhere in the state. Harry Russell, a representative and associate of the Outfit, was sent to Miami shortly afterward to oversee their new market. By the time Lefty was getting into trouble back home in the early 1960s, Miami was very much still influenced by the Outfit. Given this, it's not surprising that Miami was the city Lefty turned to for a brighter future when Illinois seemed to turn on him.

Lefty needed to be able to start fresh, in a place where the police wouldn't constantly be harassing and targeting him. In 1961, after his arrest, he moved to Miami. At first, Lefty played it safe, which was the right move. He wasn't even close to giving up gambling, but the operation he started in Miami was significantly smaller than the one he had been operating in Chicago. The plays he was making were small, and he wasn't involved as much with Mafia activity, which included tipping off gangsters to hot plays or fixed games. In this way, he managed to avoid the heat that had haunted him back home. But Lefty wasn't just a hobbyist or a part-time gambler. He was a professional, and this was what he was born to do. It didn't take long for Lefty to get tired of just being a small-time player. Before long, he was running another massive operation in Florida. He had gone back to his old habit of betting on several games at once, and they weren't small wagers. At his peak in Miami, he would often be dropping tens of thousands of dollars on a given game. These were the games he was most confident about, and unsurprisingly, he was very successful. There was an old saying around the Chicago gambling underworld that pointed out how disadvantaged the players were when taking bets against the house: "in the winter, the bookies go to Florida and the players eat snowballs." Lefty managed to prove otherwise, moving to Florida while still winning big as a player.

Lefty's business was picking up nicely again, but not everything was going smoothly in the south. Lefty, of course, had a national reputation at this point, but in Miami, he simply didn't have the extensive connections that he possessed in Chicago. Perhaps seeing Lefty as a kind of fish out of water, it didn't take long for some local tough guys to come along, demanding that he pay them a tribute for being able to operate in their territory. Local gangsters knew who he was, and they knew his earning potential. Having a guy like Frank Rosenthal paying you a share of his winnings meant very big pay days. Perhaps the most distressing of these local wise guys was a man known simply as "Eli." He was apparently just a street-level guy, but he had friends in high places and one day, he tried shaking Lefty down for regular cash payments. Both Lefty and Eli had big egos, and as adamantly as Eli insisted on Lefty bowing down, Lefty refused in kind. It's important to remember that although Chicago police were at the time renowned for being easily bought, corruption was not unique to Chicago law enforcement. There were plenty of Miami police that were on one gangster or another's payroll, and Eli had important ones. As retribution for refusing to pay tribute, the Miami thug pulled some strings and got Miami PD to issue a search warrant against Lefty. When the warrant was served, police burst into Lefty's temporary home and found him on the phone, placing sports bets in his pajamas.

Lefty was arrested, but luckily, nothing much seemed to come of it. Yet again, he had escaped the grasp of the federal crusade against organized gamblers. Still, he was basically back in the same position he was in back in Chicago—he was now a target in Miami. A little while after this happened, Lefty found himself in another potentially dangerous confrontation with law enforcement. He was pulled over while driving by an unmarked car, which turned out to be driven by federal agents. They knew who Lefty was, and they had been tailing him for some time. Lefty was being unwisely confrontational with the agents, and they ended up getting into a heated disagreement. The agents had pulled Lefty over on an isolated county road at night, with woods on either side of the road. Being in such a secluded area, anything could have happened, and the agents supposedly threatened to beat him several times. Although Lefty did not necessarily believe in luck or chance, there are few other words to describe what happened next. The man that came to Lefty's rescue was none other than Tony Spilotro, the Outfit enforcer he had known since he was a child.

Tony had not relocated to Miami permanently, but at the time he was making frequent trips to Florida. Since Lefty relocated, Tony was making even more trips down south, travelling to Miami several times per year. Illegal gambling still comprised a large portion of Tony's earning power in the Outfit, and he still relied heavily on Lefty's handicapping and knowledge of the games. On the night Lefty was pulled over on that county road, Tony just happened to be driving down the same route, and when he recognized Lefty's car pulled over and saw Lefty being harassed on the side of the road, he immediately knew he had to step in. Even though he knew the men accosting him were officers, Tony was ballsy enough to bring his car to a screeching halt, hop out, and confront the men. Tony called them out for harassing an innocent person, and even taunted them, claiming that "you two gutless sonofabitches ain't gonna do nothing to him," (Pileggi, 1995). Lefty was far from home, but he still had protectors, and Tony was always the fiercest. Eventually the two agents gave up and drove off, knowing full well they were threatening someone who hadn't committed a crime. After this incident, Lefty and Tony grew closer.

Lefty was bailed out yet again, but in the long run, he clearly didn't learn any important lessons from Chicago. Over the following years in Miami, Lefty was constantly in the company of made men in the Outfit and connected guys from Florida, and he hung around guys like future Outfit boss Jackie "the lackey" Cerone, the right-hand man of then-boss Sam Giancana. He also maintained his connections with one of his old mentors, West Side boss Fiore

Buccieri, who made frequent trips down to Miami to visit Lefty. Even all the way across the country, Lefty was still one of the Chicago Mafia's most valuable assets, and they didn't want to lose him. Even though Lefty personally claimed that he moved to Florida as a kind of "free agent" outside the grip of the mob, not much changed about how or with whom he conducted his business. As a result of his continued Mafia connections, the violence followed him south. At one point he even got caught up in a gang war as the Outfit and their allies feuded with the Cuban gangs over control of Miami's organized gambling rackets. The conflict became known in Miami as the "bookie wars," which was an appropriate name considering it evolved into all-out warfare involving shootouts, frequent car bombings, and retaliations. It was a violent conflict, but it was often overshadowed at the time considering that the influx of narcotics into the southern United States in the 1960s was becoming a much more serious issue.

The 1960s was also an era of anti-Mafia crusaders. Powerful politicians like Attorney General Robert F. Kennedy, brother of then-President John F. Kennedy, dedicated their careers to upending the influence and power of organized crime in America, particularly the Mafia and their subsidiaries. One of their main tactics was to instruct law enforcement agencies to aggressively pursue guys "on the inside" of crime who may be willing to flip and become a witness or act as a secret informant in exchange for lighter prison sentences for whatever crimes they may have committed. This is the strategy that led to some of the greatest hits against organized crime in American history, especially after wise guys started getting hit with prison sentences of decades rather than months or years. When facing the prospect of dying in prison, it wasn't a hard decision for mobsters to rat out their pals. When it came to Lefty, there was nothing he had done that could've landed him such an extreme sentence, but that didn't stop federal agents from trying to recruit him. While he was in Miami, at some point after his initial arrest, he was approached again by federal agents looking to cut a deal. They wanted Lefty to feed them info on his Outfit buddies, but Lefty supposedly refused to be a rat, insisting that he was never involved in organized crime in Miami or Chicago, nor was he involved in anything illegal related to gambling. As a result of his non-cooperation, Lefty was soon after hit with a subpoena to testify before a Senate subcommittee on illegal gambling.

The subcommittee was organized by John L. McClellan, a US Senator from Arkansas who, like Robert Kennedy, was attempting to build a legacy by taking down the American Mafia. Lefty cooperated with the subpoena and actually made the trip to testify before the committee, but he hilariously refused to answer a single one of their 37 questions for him, instead invoking his Fifth Amendment right to refuse to answer questions each and every time. Among other things, he was asked if he ever worked for Angelini and Kaplan, whether he was acquainted with Fifi Buccieri or Sam Giancana, and if he ever bribed college athletes. Each time his response was simply "I decline to answer on the grounds that my answer may tend to incriminate me," (quoted in Pileggi, 1995). Even the most benign questions went unanswered. He was asked whether he had ever played baseball, and even whether he was left-handed. It didn't matter, his answer was always the same. Needless to say, the Senate did not get much information of value out of Lefty, and again, nothing much came of the investigation. Lefty stayed a free man, but a free man with a target on his back, who was now on the radars of the most powerful lawmakers in the nation.

A year later, things were getting even more intense as notable gangster-gamblers from around the country were being rounded up by the dozens. Even Gil Beckley, the man that avoided notoriety and legal attention at all costs was not spared the wrath of these crusaders. Things were also taking a downturn for Lefty. Even though he was not sitting in prison, he was hit with several restrictions that hampered his business. He was personally barred from owning any racehorses and had been issued a blanket ban from every single racetrack in the state of Florida. The government also issued a ban against communication of any and all information related to gambling across state lines, a restriction which severely crippled the bookies' ability to stay up to date. Unbeknownst to Lefty at the time, the FBI had also placed listening devices in his apartment and over the course of the next year, he was arrested several times with whatever the cops could charge him with. Still lucky as ever, none of the charges led to anything serious, but life was certainly getting more complicated for a crooked Miami bookie.

So, he had been arrested several times, hounded, threatened, and harassed by the feds, hauled before the US Senate, and forced out of his home state, all within the space of just a few years. In 1962, however, his tenure in Miami took a massive turn for the worse. That year, he received an indictment from the state of South Carolina. He was being brought up on charges of attempting to bribe a young college basketball player from New York University to shave points off of a game against North Carolina. Based on the stern advice of his legal team, Lefty ended up pleading no contest to the charges, and was subsequently convicted. Pleading no contest essentially means that you do not admit guilt to the crime, but that you do not wish to fight the charges and will simply accept the judgement of the court. There is not much information available on exactly what Lefty's sentence entailed or whether he spent much time in jail, but his decision to not contest the charges certainly saved him from a lengthy prison sentence. It appears that Lefty continued to fight for his freedom for years after his conviction (this kind of hard-headedness in the face of persecution was one of Lefty's defining traits), but these were only the beginning of his troubles. He was also at that time under intense investigation for alleged connections to a series of car bombings in the Miami area that took place during the bookie wars. If *these* investigations panned out for the police, there wasn't much hope of Lefty avoiding a prison cell again. It seemed that perhaps the best thing for him was to once again make a run for the hills and find a new place to operate.

CHAPTER 4

VIVA MOB VEGAS

As the 1960s progressed, Lefty was still holding out hope of being able to redevelop his gambling and fixing operation. He certainly didn't want to have to relocate and start anew all over again, but he soon wouldn't have much of a choice. The reality is that the entire organized crime landscape was changing before Lefty and Tony's eyes. In nearly every major city, it was getting harder to live as a mobster. It was still possible to bribe police, but the days of having entire departments in your pocket were all but dead. The mob's political connections were becoming less valuable as the government became less tolerant of corruption, and the FBI was being awoken from its stupor and being forced to actually treat organized crime as a threat to American society. The Mafia was still a powerful organization, but Lefty's pals wouldn't be able to protect him when federal agents finally decided to make their death blow. Few Mafia "sanctuaries" still existed in the country, and there was only one city in the world that still looked attractive to a guy like Lefty Rosenthal.

An Oasis in the Desert

In 1967, the Florida and federal law enforcement agencies' campaign against Lefty was paying off in a very big way. He still wasn't bound for prison, but the efforts of the government had rendered Lefty's ability to do business in Florida (and almost anywhere else) almost non-existent. Western Union, the corporation that supplied the wire service to Lefty and allowed cash payments to be transferred around the country, had officially cut him off and denied him access to the wire. Worse, the telephone company that serviced the building he lived in also cut him off, removing their phone lines from his home and refusing him telephone access. It was widely known that Lefty and his comrades were using these services to conduct illegal activity, and no company wanted to be the one that allowed it to happen using their services. Lefty was now destitute, left without the ability to transfer or receive money or information about the games outside of the state of Florida. Miami, long considered to be one of America's havens for gamblers, was now a brutally hostile environment for odds fixers. There was virtually no way for Lefty to continue his business successfully, and while Lefty had been considering abandoning Miami for a while, he now had no choice.

Shortly after Lefty lost Western Union's services, he was gone. Initially, he went back home to Chicago's West Side to try to reconnect with his old pals at the core of the Outfit. He wanted to try to restart his operation from scratch while maintaining his connections around the country. Unfortunately, Chicago hadn't become much more welcoming toward gambling kingpins since Lefty first fled years ago. It was still difficult to conduct any real operations in Chicago itself, and in fact, most of Lefty's operation was based out of Las Vegas, the casino-clad oasis in the middle of the Nevada desert, over 1,500 miles away from Chicago. All Lefty was really doing in Chicago was relaying orders to the guys in Vegas that were working for him and having information relayed back to him. He had a solid support base in his hometown, but with the gambling landscape as crippled as it was, he was essentially a fish out of water. It didn't take long for Lefty to realize that if he was going to really commit himself to the gambling lifestyle and to creating an empire, he needed to go to where the action was. He needed to go to the desert.

So, Lefty soon found himself packing up and prepping for a move to the other side of the United States to strike it big in Vegas. No longer would he be isolated from the action. Now he would be there, on the floors himself, making it happen. This was going to give him a lot more direct control over his business, plus he wouldn't have nearly as much legal trouble to worry about (or so he thought). While most of the country was turning ever more hostile to gambling racketeers, Las Vegas was filled with guys like Lefty. There, his lifestyle was accepted, and his vocation was the only game in town. The laws surrounding gambling there were as lax as they come, and the metropolitan police were still, for the most part, notoriously corrupt. There was a good chance for a guy like Lefty to get a real fresh start there, because more than anything, he just wanted to gamble. It also didn't hurt that the Outfit had a strong, long-lasting presence in the city that could guarantee Lefty's safety and market.

The day Lefty was set to leave Chicago, Tony picked him up to take him to the airport. But first, the two drove to go see Fiore Buccieri, one of Lefty's oldest mentors, so he could say his goodbyes. In reality though, neither Lefty nor the Outfit bosses had any intention of really ending their relationship. In fact, Lefty's ties to the Chicago mob only grew stronger during his time in Vegas, as he soon became one of their most profitable earners and most valuable assets. Lefty and Fifi spoke for some time, talking about their history together and of Lefty's future in Nevada. Apparently, their goodbye ran a little long, as Tony had to rush him to the airport to catch his flight. On their drive there, Tony decided to give Lefty a little taste of what he was leaving behind in Chicago. As the story goes, Tony sped so fast in his car on the way to the airport that they ended up getting into a multi-car chase with the Chicago PD. Tony eventually lost the cops chasing him and was able to hurriedly dump Lefty off without a proper goodbye before he sped off again to safety. Frankly, Lefty was terrified, and he was happy to be leaving Chicago for greener pastures and the promise of being able to make it big in a new, more welcoming home.

Some sources claim that Lefty had initially gone to Las Vegas as a "freelancer," and indeed that he operated solo for years after he arrived. His persistent ties to the bosses in Chicago, however, tell a much different story. Plus, it would have been very difficult to operate 100% independently in a city like Las Vegas, because like Miami, the Outfit had a very long history in the city. Back in 1943, when Outfit bosses Paul Ricca and Frank Nitti were charged in relation to union racketeering and extortion out in California on the west coast, the Family began looking very strongly at Las Vegas. It was very much still a virgin city at the time, and it had a lot of promise. It was the perfect target for expansion, as other Families from across the country also began moving out to the desert. Bugsy Siegel already controlled a large casino operation in the city, and from 1933 onwards he had been a strong ally of the Outfit. Chicago provided Siegel with support and protection in exchange for a big cut of the action. By the mid-1940s, though, Siegel had become a problem for many of his associates, including Chicago, as it appeared very likely that he had started skimming from the Mafia's cut. Siegel's Flamingo Hotel was one of the mob's biggest and most reliable cash cows, and they couldn't tolerate it being mismanaged or left in the hands of an unpredictable thief. In 1947, Siegel was gunned down from a distance while inside his girlfriend's mansion in Beverly Hills. His murder remains a mystery to this day, but what is known is that at the time of his death he was meeting with an associate from the Outfit, and almost immediately after his assassination, one of the Outfit's representatives in Las Vegas named Gus Greenbaum staged a hostile takeover of the Flamingo, seizing it for the Outfit directly.

After Siegel was gone, the Outfit continued to profit off of Las Vegas' rackets. Salvatore "Sam" Giancana, who became boss in the late 1950s, was a very big player in the gambling scene, and he profited massively off of the Outfit's operations in Vegas. He also had no problem exercising Chicago's power and influence over the city's casinos. He had enough clout to demand that Vegas establishments install slot machines manufactured in Chicago, in factories that Giancana had an interest in. Few operations in the city were bold enough to refuse, and so Illinois machines flooded the market. Giancana, of course, profited directly from this. He got paid once when the slot machines were built, and then again when they were purchased and installed in any one of Vegas' lavish resort-style gambling establishments. Marshall Caifano, a high-ranking Outfit guy throughout the 1940s and 50s, was also a huge presence in Las Vegas and across the West Coast. In the 1940s he was sent to maintain Chicago's presence in Los Angeles, and in fact, it was Caifano's associate Alan Smiley that was present at Bugsy Siegel's girlfriend's home when the casino mogul was shot to death. For a long time, Caifano was the Outfit's main guy on the Vegas Strip, overseeing and protecting their interests there for years, and supervising the incredibly lucrative "skim" operation. That is, until Caifano was replaced by someone even more vicious...

So, Lefty's journey to the oasis in the desert was not a first for the Outfit. Still, having someone with his talents in that city could be a game-changer. If he could manage to keep his nose clean, that is. Unfortunately, Lefty was already generating a lot of buzz in "Sin City" even before his plane touched down at Harry Reid International Airport. Chicago police and the city's crime commission had obviously been keeping very close tabs on Lefty since his surprising arrival back in Chicago from Miami, so it was no surprise that they were well aware of his intentions to move to Nevada even before Lefty had committed to the decision. Plus, the crime commission had been maintaining a strong relationship with Vegas Metro police for years by this point, helping them to keep tabs on known Mafiosi who were operating in the city. As soon as the rumors of Lefty's big move to the desert were confirmed, Chicago police quickly forwarded their entire profile on Lefty and his history to officials in Nevada. This included all the details of his extensive rap sheets, which came with a glaring lack of convictions.

Las Vegas was warned that Lefty was on his way and that trouble was not too far behind.

Before the West Side bookie extraordinaire stepped off his trans-America flight, the Las Vegas police already knew everything about him. He didn't even have to show his face for them to recognize him. They knew about his arrests in Chicago. They knew about his affinity for bribing sports players and referees, and they knew about his shady connections, including with Tony "the Ant" Spilotro. They knew about his stay in Miami and the indictments he received there. They even knew about his infamous "I decline to answer" debacle at the McClellan committee hearings. Lefty was, at that moment, very likely recalling the wise words of Gil Beckley, and wishing he had done more to follow them. He couldn't stay out of the spotlight, and he refused to distance himself from the Chicago Mafia. Both of these decisions were coming back to haunt him in a big way. The noise he had raised in both Illinois and Florida had clearly done some serious damage, and it left him virtually no hope of making a true fresh start in Vegas, or anywhere else for that matter. He was a known guy, a person of interest, and the term "low profile," may as well have dropped right out of Lefty's vocabulary.

When it became clear that Lefty intended on staying in Vegas long term, it didn't take long for the Metro police to make their first move. Having only been in the city for a few days, Lefty received a knock on the door at the place where he was staying, sometime in the morning or afternoon. On the other side was Gene Clark, the chief of the Las Vegas police. Clark obviously wasn't there to welcome Lefty, nor was he there simply to give a stern warning. He came with an ultimatum. Lefty was to immediately pack up all of the belongings he had brought with him and catch the next flight straight back to Chicago. In those days, there weren't many flights directly between Vegas and Chicago. Clark advised him that the earliest one was leaving at midnight that night, and that would be his only chance. Lefty was going to be on the plane, and if he wasn't, Clark threatened him with death. Las Vegas was a city where even the Mafia didn't like to make trouble. At least, not within the city limits. When someone needed to be disposed of, they were taken out into Nevada's vast Mojave Desert, far away from civilization, executed and then buried. This was a known habit of Las Vegas gangsters, and the desert had earned a sinister reputation for how many bodies were believed to have been buried out there. If Lefty wasn't on that midnight flight out of the city, Clark assured him that Lefty's body would be the next one filling a hole.

Lefty didn't seem to have been deterred. He made no immediate plans to book the flight, instead deciding to seek counsel from some of his Outfit connections in Vegas. Vegas police had a reputation for being extremely corrupt, and so one piece of advice Lefty received was to simply pay Clark off. Some advised him to ignore the police chief altogether, because he wasn't going to follow through on anything. It would have been a good idea to lay low for a while, but that ship had long since sailed. All the advice he received was pointless anyway, as Clark apparently didn't feel like waiting. With no clear signs that Lefty was heeding his warning and preparing to leave, Clark got a few of his officers together and confronted Lefty yet again, a few hours before the midnight deadline. They told him there was no way he was going to make his flight if he didn't pick up the pace and get ready. Apparently, Clark and his men were there to help with that process. Under Clark's orders, the officers essentially kidnapped the Chicago bookie and drove him to the airport. They escorted him through the airport before forcing him to board the plane bound for Illinois. Lefty literally did not have a choice in the matter, and so off he went. Just like that, it seemed that Lefty's tenure in Las Vegas was going to be over before it even got started.

Lefty found himself back in Chicago yet again, unplanned and against his will. Still, he wasn't quite ready to give up. While in Illinois, Lefty once again sought the counsel of some Outfit friends of his. The most level-headed advice he received was from an acquaintance who was quite familiar with the Las Vegas scene. He explained to Lefty that guys like Chief Gene Clark really had no other choice than to do what he did. He had to act like a tough guy, to flex his muscles a little bit. Apparently, it was all for appearances. Someone like Clark had to at least give the impression that he was tough on crime, so the drastic actions he took against Lefty were really all just to prove a point. In reality, Las Vegas at the time was still as crooked a city as they make them, and the local cops were more than willing to look the other way in exchange for a cut of the action. With that, Lefty was soon booking yet another flight out to the desert to once again make an attempt at becoming a citizen of Nevada. Whether or not the advice Lefty received was really true of Clark's motivations, it appears that Lefty didn't have any long history with the chief and didn't even have many run-ins with him after the first confrontation. This time Lefty took up residence at the Tropicana Hotel, a very important location in the saga of Lefty Rosenthal. There, he would meet someone that was going to change his life forever.

A Match Made in Vegas

The Tropicana Hotel opened its doors in 1957, and from the beginning, it was closely affiliated with the Mafia. It was a lavish and ritzy resort-style hotel that featured a large adjoining casino and nearly 1,500 guest rooms. At the time of its opening, it was Las Vegas' most expensive casino project and set a high standard for future projects. By the late 1960s when Lefty became a resident, it was facing stiff competition from larger casinos, but it was still a mostly successful establishment. Since 1959 it had been home to *Les Folies Bergere*, a large and world-famous entertainment show that featured topless showgirls and dancers. It eventually became the longest-running show in Las Vegas' history, and it turns out that Lefty himself was a big fan of the provocative dancers. He took a liking to several of them, but none more than one girl named Geri McGee. Lefty wasn't the only one with eyes on Geri, however. She was easily one of the most popular dancers in the entire city, and this meant that she was very accustomed to getting what she wanted. The question was whether or not she wanted Lefty.

Geri, of course, didn't spend all her time at the Tropicana. In addition to being a topless showgirl, she was also a notorious "chip hustler." Basically, a chip hustler was a woman who would hang around betting tables, using their good looks and charisma to flirt with the high rollers. Craps players would often have them blow on dice, believing it was a kind of lucky charm, or sometimes they would have them call out lucky numbers to determine their bets. When the players they hung around with lost these bets, the girls usually just washed their hands of it, laughed it off, and left to go look for another sucker. But when the numbers they called or the dice they blew on won, they expected (and sometimes demanded) a cut of the winnings. When Geri wasn't dancing or spending time with her daughter Robin, she could be found at any one of Vegas' most exclusive establishments, schmoozing and hanging around with the big spenders. The men would take her shopping, buy her the most expensive jewelry, take her to the finest restaurants and clubs, and even give her weekly allowances, all just to have her around. She had plenty of guys that she did this with, and men would take trips out to Vegas from all over the country just to see Geri. There were plenty of girls in Vegas who made careers out of flirting with rich men, but Geri was easily one of the most in-demand women in the city. She, like many others, would also sleep with several of the men that treated her the best, but that was reserved for the highest of high rollers.

Perhaps it was the fact that Geri was the desire of half the men in Las Vegas that Lefty took such a shining to her. No one had ever locked her down for very long, but everyone wanted to, and maybe that was a challenge for the guy who always wanted to be the best at everything he did. Whatever the reason, Lefty had his eyes on Geri since the day he first saw her dancing up on the stage of the glamorous Tropicana Hotel in the famous *Folies Bergere*. But he didn't truly fall in love with her until he saw her in action, chip hustling on the casino floor. He was awe-struck at how well she gamed the men. She flirted just enough to get them to think she wanted them but held out just enough to get them to drop a ton of cash on her. Her methods were not always so innocent, though. Besides just expecting tips from the guys whose arms she clung to at the blackjack tables, Geri liked to hedge her bets by sneaking stray chips into her purse or bra whenever no one was looking. She actually got quite good at sleight of hand, and she was an expert at concealing chips in the palms of her hands. One night though, this got Geri into a bit of trouble, and Lefty was there to witness it all.

While Geri was chip hustling one night, she linked up with a man at one of the tables who was not one of her regular marks. She had spent a few hours with him, and he was having some particularly good luck, except for the fact that Geri had been pocketing his chips behind his back the entire night. Or at least, she thought it was behind his back. In reality, the man had caught her several times sneaking them into her purse, but he just didn't call her out. At the end of the night, when Geri and the man were getting ready to part ways, she pressed her luck. Offended that the man simply started to walk away without giving her a generous tip, Geri called him out for being cheap and insisted that he cough up some chips. This was the last straw—the man accused her of stealing more than enough chips from him already and demanded that she give back what she took. To escape the situation, Geri did the only thing that someone like Geri would do in that event. She grabbed a huge stack of the man's chips and launched them into the air and scattered them across the casino floor. Other gamblers (and even the casino security guards) rushed over to try to pocket as many chips as they could amidst the shouting and chaos, and the man who accused Geri was too busy trying to stop everyone from stealing his chips to even think about pursuing her. So, Geri made a quick and easy escape, laughing all the way while Lefty stood at a distance and admired her. There, Lefty Rosenthal fell in love.

Geri had a really great scam going in Las Vegas. She was very successful, owned her own expensive home, and was able to support her, her daughter, and even her family back in California on the money she earned, which was somewhere around half a million dollars per year. She was always very good at making money, and she understood the city of Las Vegas like few others did. Many folks from all over came and went from the city every year, staying for weeks or months at a time, or sometimes years. But Geri made that city her home since she moved there from her native California. By the time Lefty first arrived in the desert, Geri had already been there for eight years, laying roots and learning how to squeeze money out of her marks. Surprisingly though, it wasn't even Geri's idea to move there in the first place. Apparently, she was pressured into going to Sin City by a man named Lenny Marmor, who was an old boyfriend of hers from her days in California. He also happened to be the father of Geri's daughter Robin. Marmor was essentially just a petty criminal, pimp, and an overall slimy person, but she undoubtedly loved him. She had relationships with plenty of men in Vegas, but Marmor was the one she never forgot. He had convinced Geri that there were a lot of suckers in Vegas and that she would be able to make a ton of money to be able to support her family back home. In reality though, Marmor was probably hoping that Geri would make the cash by whoring herself out and that he would receive his cut of her profit. She was almost certainly being exploited, but she ended up the winner in the situation, as she was quite a wealthy woman by the time Lefty arrived in 1968, while Marmor was still skating by as a low life street-level pimp.

When Geri first came out to the city to make a new life for herself, she started off as a dancer and eventually found herself at the luxurious Tropicana. There was certainly decent money in it, especially considering the tips from the hotel and casino patrons (even though the Tropicana wasn't necessarily where all the biggest spenders went), but Geri quickly realized that there was much more money to be made in a city like Las Vegas where men were willing to drop their life savings pursuing their pleasures and desires. She started hitting the casino floors and getting acclimated to the real landscape of the city. She'd head out with her better-paying clients at the end of her shifts at the Tropicana to accompany them while they blew even more money at the tables. Just like Lefty did, Geri learned what made the betters tick. She learned their habits, she learned when they spent and when they didn't, and she learned how to get them to spend more. She learned how to manipulate these men as well as Lefty learned how to manipulate the odds they were betting with. And just like Lefty, Geri proved to be a natural at it. By the time Lefty first saw her performing at the Tropicana, Geri was basically only dancing for tax purposes. She needed to be able to declare some sort of legal income on her taxes and show the government that she held gainful employment. Her *real* income was made almost exclusively through hustling for casino chips and partying with the high-stakes gamers who enjoyed showering her with gifts and cash.

Unsurprisingly, Lefty really liked this about her. She was a lot like him, and they were both after the same thing. They were both immersed in, and understood, the world of gambling. They both made a living by taking advantage of the players and always tilting the odds in their favor. Both of them seemed destined to make it big in a place like Sin City. Most importantly, they were both always on the hunt for another sucker. Lefty didn't want to be her next sucker, though. He wanted a relationship with her, but would she ever see him as more than another mark? Another piggy bank? He was in love, but he knew what love meant to a working girl, especially one as desirable and high maintenance as Geri McGee. She was the forbidden fruit that the whole city seemed to want but that no one could ever have for more than a few nights at a time. The odds were slim that Lefty would ever be able to lock her down, but Lefty had been trying to beat the odds since he was a kid. And not to mention the fact that Lefty was, frankly, unlike any other guy that Geri had ever dealt with.

Lefty started out as just another customer of hers, but he was persistent. He treated her the best, got her whatever she wanted, and discouraged her from seeing other guys or going out on her own to patrol the tables for suckers. Still, she didn't see anything in him at first besides a source of cash. She still did her own thing, and Lefty continued to try to lock her down. One thing that Lefty picked up on rather quickly, however, was the fact that Geri's true love had always been, and probably would always be, money. He knew about Lenny Marmor, Robin's father and Geri's ex-boyfriend from back home, but Lefty knew that even he took a backseat to Geri's love for money. She loved the extravagance it could bring to her lifestyle, and she loved the independence that it gave her. But most importantly, it allowed her to care for her daughter and the rest of her family. She earned more than enough for herself, and she didn't mind using the rest to support the ones she loved. That came before everything else, no matter how much Lefty tried to make her his own. Cash is what motivated her, day in and day out, and like so many others in Las Vegas (including Lefty), it occupied nearly 100% of her thoughts. Lefty later recalled that "to her, a night was a waste if she didn't go home with cash in her pocket," (Pileggi, 1995). Lefty knew he would never be her priority, but that didn't stop him from trying.

The two eventually began an actual, honest relationship, but Geri was always hesitant to let him get too close. Even having left Lenny back in California so many years ago, it still felt like she was cheating on him. He was really the only guy she had been very close with. And besides, Geri was right to be on guard. Despite her confidence, she was a vulnerable woman with a troubled past. She actually shared quite a few similarities with the famously tortured celebrity, Marilyn Monroe. Besides the fact that they were both stunningly attractive and free-spirited, they both grew up in California and both attended Van Nuys High School (Geri about a decade after Marilyn), but most importantly, they both had mothers that struggled terribly with severe mental illness which had a lasting effect on the rest of their lives. Indeed, Geri was Lefty's "blonde bombshell." Over time, he continued to fall more in love with her, but Geri didn't seem to reciprocate. As Lefty recalled, "She didn't give it much thought... I don't think it even dawned on Geri that I was beginning to feel differently about her," (quoted in Pileggi, 1995).

Still, Geri was indeed seeing other guys less, and it had become a known thing around town that Geri and Lefty were dating. Lefty was still on his own during the day, figuring out his bets and making the right calls to the right people to get it all done, and meanwhile Geri was still dancing at the Tropicana and meeting up with her usual marks after her shift, but when all that was done, Geri and Lefty were together, hitting the town as a couple with plenty of cash in their pockets. Their relationship continued on for some months, all the while Lefty's love and affection went unrequited. Lefty made it known to Geri that he intended on marrying her, but she didn't share his enthusiasm. She was always hesitant about the whole idea, especially because she had spent the last several years of her life being completely independent (in fact, she had gotten used to people being dependent on her, not the other way around). Lefty wanted to make an honest woman out of her, he wanted her to settle down with him. Needless to say, that would have been a jarring change in Geri's life. So even after months of dating, she kept Lefty at arm's length. She eventually sought the counsel of some of her friends and family. Some told her to simply stay away from a guy like Lefty, but some tried to convince her to marry him anyway, because they knew how wealthy he was. She would simply have to wait a while, then divorce him. She would be legally entitled to half his money, and then she could actually afford to give up her transient lifestyle without having to settle as a housewife for someone she didn't love. It was a tempting prospect, but she still had her reservations. Apparently, Geri was a big believer in horoscopes and birth signs, and because Lefty was a Gemini, she thought he was inherently untrustworthy and incompatible with her.

At the same time, Lefty was also being cautioned by his own friends in the city who knew he planned on proposing to her. These were guys who had been around Las Vegas for a long time and knew what Geri was like. For a guy like Lefty who was trying to avoid attention after being forced out of both Illinois and Florida, Geri was the wrong woman for him. She was big trouble just waiting to happen, and neither Lefty nor his partners needed that kind of stress in their lives. They told him she would never actually settle down with him, that she would never love him. They said she was just a call girl and that she was only hanging around with Lefty in the first place because of his bank account. They told him that even if he wanted to be with her, he had to keep her away. Geri McGee was a woman who could ruin everything. Still, Lefty was undeterred by the counsel of his friends. At the same time, Geri, for some reason or another, apparently changed her mind about the prospect of a marriage engagement. On May 1 of 1969, just one year after Lefty Rosenthal first arrived in the desert, he and Geri McGee were husband and wife. Even despite the fact that Geri said yes to his proposal, Lefty was under no illusions. She still didn't love him. It wasn't *true* love, at least. But that didn't matter. Lefty was convinced that he would be able to build a relationship with her. He believed that given enough time, he would be able to wear down her tough exterior that she had built up after years of hustling on the Las Vegas Strip. He believed he would make an honest woman out of her, and that he could build a healthy, happy family together with her. He thought he could *make* her love him. As we'll see later in Lefty's story, this didn't work out exactly as planned.

CHAPTER 5

A HOLE IN THE WALL

By the end of 1969, Lefty was a married man, Geri McGee had (seemingly) settled down as a wife with her daughter Robin beside her, and the city of Las Vegas was becoming accustomed to the presence of the man who was arguably the nation's #1 handicapper and odds fixer. Lefty did not yet have a big operation, and he was not even close to reaching the peak of his power in Nevada, but his arrival had made waves, nonetheless. He was a full-time gambler, and his wagers were consistently large and consistently correct. He was earning enough to surround both himself and Geri with every luxury they could ever want, and things were looking quite good for the Rosenthals. Las Vegas was still a city where just about anyone could operate freely, the mob had an interest in keeping the city core safe, and police interference was negligible, for the most part. But besides that, Lefty wasn't doing anything particularly questionable, so neither Las Vegas Metro nor the FBI had much reason to come down on him. Meanwhile, Tony "the Ant" Spilotro was still back in Chicago. At least for the moment.

A Little Off the Top

In 1969, Tony Spilotro already had a reputation as being incredibly violent, ruthless, and ambitious. These same qualities eventually led to his downfall (and, in fact, the downfall of the entire Mafia's presence in Las Vegas), but for the time being, these were the kinds of characteristics that allowed someone to climb the ladder of organized crime. Being implicated in the so-called "M&M Murders" had made him even more vicious in public opinion, and the fact that he was implicated alongside Mad Sam DeStefano was huge for his underworld credibility. Sources differ on what exactly occurred during the murders. Some claim that one of the robbers was tortured until he gave up the location of the other, and some sources claim they were both captured and tortured at the same time. Regardless, the mangled and obviously tortured bodies of Bill McCarthy and Jimmy Miraglia were discovered in the trunk of a car in May 1962, and Tony Spilotro was the number one suspect.

In the case investigating his role in McCarthy and Miraglia's deaths, Tony was represented by none other than Oscar Goodman, a well-known mob lawyer who had worked to defend multiple criminals in the Las Vegas area, including the legendary Meyer Lansky as well as Herbie Blitzstein and Philly Leonetti. As a testament to how deeply the legal machinery in Nevada was connected to organized crime, Oscar Goodman also later became Mayor of Las Vegas. It would take some years before Tony would face any kind of real justice for his brutal crimes in Chicago, but the heat was already starting to burn him. It was beginning to look like Tony might have to go the way of Lefty and get the hell out of Dodge. Tony had been out to Vegas several times recently both to see Lefty and to attend to Outfit business, but his main operation was still very much in Illinois. During one of his trips to the desert, however, he at some point asked Lefty an important question. He wanted his opinion on whether or not Tony should consider moving out there as well. Lefty didn't want to upset Tony, but he wasn't exactly enthusiastic about that possibility. Tony was exactly the kind of person that Lefty wanted to leave behind in Chicago, and he was exactly the type of person who could mess up whatever Lefty had built in Vegas by that point. Lefty was noncommittal in his response, but it didn't matter. Vegas was on Tony's mind.

Luckily for Tony Spilotro, there was indeed a vacancy that needed to be filled by the Outfit out in Las Vegas. The Sicilian-born gangster Marshall Caifano had for a long time been representing the Outfit's interests on the West Coast, including Nevada and California. His tenure in the West stretched back to the Vegas days of Bugsy Siegel, so he was a seasoned veteran with plenty of experience in the city. Unfortunately, it became much more difficult for Caifano to oversee business there in 1960, even though he had become a powerful and high-ranking mafioso in the Chicago mob. That year, the Gaming Control Board of Nevada released a list containing the names of 11 well-known organized criminals who operated in the city of Las Vegas. Officially named the List of Excluded Persons, it was more commonly known as the Black Book, and it contained the names of two Chicago-based mobsters. The first was boss Sam Giancana, and the other was Marshall Caifano. Being on this list meant that you were not allowed, under any circumstances, to be found inside of *any* Las Vegas gambling establishment. These names belonged to men who were identified by the state as individuals very likely to be involved in illegal operations, and it was believed that making it illegal for them to be inside casinos would cripple their ability to operate. In Caifano's case, it was indeed a hindrance. It became far more difficult for him to oversee the Outfit's casino businesses, but he still lingered in the city for a few years. Later in the 1960s, however, Caifano came under legal trouble for extortion allegations, and in 1966 he was off to prison.

After Caifano was put away, the Outfit's presence in Vegas was weakened. They still had plenty of men in the city, but none with the power and influence that Caifano had. The position of "overseer" was vacant, and the bosses wanted someone out there to protect the business and make sure none of their guys decided to go rogue. The top Outfit brass eventually selected Tony "the Ant" Spilotro to succeed Caifano in 1971, likely on the recommendation of Paul Ricca. This choice made sense at the time. Like Lefty, Tony was eager to get out of the city to escape the heat he had brought down upon himself there. He was also already quite immersed in the world of gambling at the time, and he understood how to make money off of it. Las Vegas, he agreed, was the best place for him to be able to do that. Plus, Tony had all the right connections that he would need to be able to make it big in the city, including being almost life-long acquaintances with Frank Rosenthal. The only real problem was a simple one: Tony was a street guy, through and through. He didn't have much tact, and he wasn't a "diplomatic" mafioso. His ruthlessness certainly made him capable of protecting the business and the Outfit's interests, but it was almost impossible for a guy like him not to make a lot of noise and draw attention to himself. In the late 1960s and early '70s, Las Vegas was not a city that needed more trouble from law enforcement. Still, it was determined he would be the best choice. In 1971, he was sent off to the desert.

Tony was soon on a plane to Las Vegas, and while he was there, he was meant to report directly back to James "Turk" Torello, a kind of manager back in Chicago. Torello was an important guy in the Outfit, and he was a good person to keep happy. He later took over the West Side after the death of Lefty's mentor Fiore Buccieri in August 1973 and was quickly becoming one of the highest-ranking Chicago mobsters. Tony of course still had guys above him that he needed to answer to, but he was given a broad foundation of power out West. He wasn't just given domain over Las Vegas, but the majority of the Outfit's Western territories, including Arizona and most of Southern California. This was a lot of responsibility, and Tony had never had control over such a vast area of influence. He held a lot of power, but apparently even this wasn't enough. Almost immediately after he landed in Las Vegas, Tony had the intention of branching out on his own and establishing a base of power out West that was all his own. That meant no answering to anybody, no bosses back in Chicago that he needed to keep happy, and no one's interests to look out for other than his own. He wanted to strike off on his own and be independent. Despite being nicknamed "the Ant," his ambitions were larger than life.

Actually, there is some dispute over how Tony acquired his famous nickname in the first place. The most obvious answer was that it began as mockery to poke fun at his unusually small stature (the man stood just a little over 5 feet tall), and some sources take this as the truth. Others claim that the term was coined by the media after noted FBI agent William F. Roemer Jr. referred to Tony as a "pissant." This was apparently too vulgar for the papers to publish, and so they omitted "piss" and simply referred to him as the "ant." However, it's equally likely that Roemer, who happened to be the same man that helped bring down infamous New York City mob boss Joseph Bonanno, only referred to Tony as a pissant because he already had the moniker "the Ant." Still other sources claim it came from FBI agents mishearing a conversation through a wiretap. Apparently, an associate of Tony's referred to him as "Anth," supposedly another shortform of the name Anthony, but it came through the wiretap as "Ant." Frank Cullotta later recalled the moment Tony apparently heard of the nickname: "'Anth' is short for 'Anthony,' but these jackoffs didn't know the difference," (Cullotta, 2017). In any case, it doesn't appear that Tony was fond of the pseudonym.

So, just like Lefty, Tony was staring wide-eyed at a city that he intended on making his own. Ostensibly, Tony was there to protect Lefty and all of the Outfit's interests in the city, but he was really there to bring the city under his heels. This would take time though. He had only just arrived and was not yet a household name in Vegas. In 1971, Tony's only mission was to make sure the bosses out East still got paid, otherwise his bid for power would be over before it even began. Above all else, Tony's mandate was to protect "the skim" at all costs. This was Marshall Caifano's mandate as well, just as it was every Outfit representative's mandate dating back to when Chicago mobsters first stepped into the city. It was by far the Mafia's most lucrative operation in the city, and it had flown under the noses of law enforcement for decades. Even in the worst of times, the cash flow from the skim needed to continue unimpeded, or there would be hell to pay. In reality, it was the only true reason the

Mafia was out there in the desert in the first place. Basically, "skimming" was the act of taking a bit of cash at a time off the top of a given casino's earnings. It involved removing cash profits directly from the casino storerooms *before* it got recorded as official income in the casino's revenue. This way, the government and law enforcement agencies wouldn't know that the money was missing, or that it was even being made. It simply vanished, like it never existed at all. Meanwhile, it was being funneled right back to Chicago.

In Vegas, everyone from top to bottom was involved in the skim, and everyone stood to profit from it. Even the money room guys who counted the cash were making bank from it. The entire process was actually quite simple. A guy would walk through the casino doors with an empty briefcase. He would waltz right into the restricted area, gain access to the vault, walk right past the counters, collect a predetermined amount of cash, and leave with a briefcase containing up to hundreds of thousands of dollars at a time. Then, he would fly back to Chicago to greet the bosses who were eager for another payday. The guys counting the money simply kept their eyes down, pretending like they didn't see anything. Besides being paid to have their blinders on, they would also casually slip bills into their pockets throughout their shift. No one cared, because everyone was winning. That is, except the players.

Operating the skim meant that the guy at the top needed to be in on it. The man running the casinos needed to be as crooked as the guy walking out of the vault every week with a very heavy briefcase. Unfortunately, it was difficult for guys with a rap sheet to be able to run, or even work in, a casino in Las Vegas. In recent years, state law had become stricter, and the government was on the lookout for anyone in a position of power who might be looking to funnel money out of the state. So-called "front men" were almost always used by the Mafia to divert attention from the guys who were actually calling the shots. These were meant to be upstanding citizens and businessmen who wouldn't arouse any suspicion. In the 1970s, for the Chicago Outfit, this front man was Allen Glick, a well-known and well-respected property developer from the San Diego area. Glick was eager to take part in the Las Vegas casino business, but as we'll see, he didn't know exactly what he was getting into when he agreed to get into business with the likes of these Chicago businessmen. The offer was too good to pass up. The Outfit had used their crooked labor union connections to secure tens of millions of dollars from the notoriously corrupt Teamsters Union. The cash was sourced from the Teamsters Pension Fund and was used to finance the purchase of four large casinos in the city. Glick was selected to be the man on top. These casinos were the Hacienda, the Marina, the Fremont, and the Stardust, the latter of which was bought in 1974 by Glick, via his Outfit connections. With Glick ostensibly in charge of the operations, everyone at nearly every level was involved in and being paid from the scam they were running, and Tony was chosen to be the man in the background who made sure it all ran smoothly. He was the iron in Glick's glove. These casinos were massive cash cows for the Outfit for many years, and it all rested on the shoulders of Tony (and soon, Lefty).

As if they didn't know what kind of man Tony Spilotro was, the bosses in Chicago told him they were strictly against him making waves in Las Vegas because they didn't want anything at all to jeopardize the skim. Even if all else failed, cash from the casinos needed to flow. Lefty had already voiced his reservations about Tony coming to Vegas and told him that Vegas police were used to getting rid of troublemakers by burying them out in the desert. He also knew that Tony would have a very difficult time refraining from committing the kind of violent crimes that would put Chicago's bottom line at risk. His counsel mattered little, however. Tony was there to stay, and he didn't plan on keeping quiet for very long.

The Gold Rush

Tony was expected not to deviate from the orders from Chicago, but he of course was still able to make his own money on the side. He had several side businesses going and he was steadily growing his Las Vegas crew to be able to assert control over the city. But he also had time to pursue some of his special interests, and his biggest special interest was jewelry. In fact, Tony had something of an obsession with anything gold or silver. Being a skilled heist man by trade, jewels were among his favorite goods to plunder. In 1971, the same year he settled in the city, he opened up a nice, small jewelry shop inside the Circus Circus Hotel and Casino on South Las Vegas Boulevard. Exactly where Tony managed to get his hands on the jewelry, he sold there isn't known for sure, but he was almost certainly using the storefront as a fence (i.e., a place to unload stolen goods). Prior to 1971, Circus Circus had been experiencing some severe financial difficulties which included crippling debt. Luckily for them, the notorious Teamsters were once again there to step up to the plate. The heavily corrupt labor union was willing to dip into its Pension Fund for yet another casino operation, and they were able to completely wipe out Circus Circus' debt. They even bankrolled the construction of a brand-new hotel portion to add onto the casino to help it become more profitable and attractive to investors. As a condition of this new deal, Circus Circus was to allow Tony to open up and run his jewelry business in their establishment.

Officially though, it wasn't Tony Spilotro that was running the shop. In an effort to avoid name recognition, the Chicago enforcer operated under the name "Tony Stuart." It was definitely a thin veil, and it certainly wasn't going to conceal him from the FBI for very long. As it turned out, the feds were keeping very close tabs on Tony's whereabouts even outside of Chicago. In fact, just as it was with Lefty, Nevada officials had been aware of Tony's expected presence in the city even before his arrival. Once he was there, it didn't take long for the FBI to catch on to what he was up to. They discovered that "Tony Stuart," the harmless ring and necklace merchant, was in fact the brutal West Side gangster Tony Spilotro, and they quickly forwarded all their information on him to Nevada law enforcement. Under the direction of the feds, they then confronted Tony about the store and strong armed him into shutting it down. For the most part, the Las Vegas Metro police and the FBI didn't exactly get along, and its not often that they would act on the commands of the FBI like this. After all, Vegas cops were notorious for accepting bribes, but the top brass in the state apparently did not like the fact that Tony was in the city, and they didn't want the kind of trouble he was expected to bring. Just like Gene Clark did when he shipped Lefty back off to Chicago, the Vegas Metro police were trying to make a point. Guys like them were not welcome. For the time being, Tony remained relatively quiet.

A little while after his confrontation with Vegas police, Tony opened up shop again in a rustic-looking wooden roadside store near Las Vegas Boulevard that he named the Gold Rush. The Gold Rush wasn't a very glamorous place, but it did earn Tony and his crew quite a handsome profit. The jewelry business actually could have been a convenient opportunity for Tony to partake in a perfectly legal and legitimate operation, which would have made it perfect for laundering his illegal income, but this wasn't the case at all. The Gold Rush's inventory was made up entirely of pieces that Tony's crew had stolen, heisted, or burgled. The group of thieves and murderers that Tony assembled who stocked the inventory of the Gold Rush came to be known as the Hole in the Wall Gang. They earned this nickname due to the fact that after they had finished up with a heist, often all that was left behind was a gaping hole in the wall they broke through to enter the building. Their breaking through walls was not due to ineptitude or poor planning, however. Apparently, many homes in the Las Vegas area at the time were built with stucco walls which were incredibly easy to break through with a sledgehammer. Plus, breaking through the wall was often a preferable route of entry anyway, because the homes' security systems, if they had one at all, would typically only be triggered by entry through a door or a window. Whatever job they were on, the Hole in the Wall Gang always had the tools to break through a wall if they needed to.

Because of their skill in the burgling trade, the Gold Rush always had a steady flow of inventory. However, Tony knew the police and the feds were already keeping an eye on him, so he needed to take care in how he did his business. He had to make sure that none of the jewelry or accessories his crew stole was able to be identified within the Gold Rush's stock. To be sure of this, they had to make the jewelry completely unidentifiable. Tony and his guys would remove the gemstones and diamonds from pieces of jewelry to place them in other pieces. On top of this, they would melt down the spare gold and silver and reforge them into different kinds of jewelry. For example, a diamond from a gold ring might get removed and placed into a pair of silver earrings, a gold bracelet might get melted down into a necklace, and so on. This way, the cops would never be able to claim for sure that any given piece of jewelry from their store was the same as one that was reported as stolen. Still there were some pieces too rare or valuable to be tampered with. These special pieces were instead taken out of state, often to California or Arizona, or even back home to Chicago, where they would be fenced later.

One of his key partners at the Gold Rush was "Fat Herb" Blitzstein, an old associate of Tony's from Chicago. With Fat Herb at his side, the whole operation seemed fool proof. As far as the cops were concerned, Tony was operating a legitimate business. Even if they suspected Tony, they couldn't prove it, so what could they do? He was convinced his crew were too professional and talented to get pinched doing a job, so they all just continued to steal with impunity. A while later, in 1979, Tony's close friend and associate Frank Cullotta was released from prison, and it didn't take long for the pair to reunite. After Frank's celebratory "getting out" party, he was soon convinced by Tony to get on a plane and fly out to the desert to team up with himself and Fat Herb. When Cullotta arrived, Tony's antics in Las Vegas rose to a new level. Tony explained his plan to Frank. He explained his intention to seize on the golden opportunity that was Las Vegas. He explained his intention to become the real big boss of the city. Tony wanted Frank to begin assembling a brand-new crew of reliable and trusted associates to take to the streets and start enforcing on his behalf. There was nothing really unusual about this request, other than the fact that Tony demanded that Frank's guys not be connected to the Chicago Outfit. Tony clearly wanted to keep some distance between this operation and his bosses in the Midwest.

Tony's plan was to move on all the independent operators that still remained in Las Vegas. The city that was once an open marketplace for criminals where no one claimed sole ownership was now being brought under the boot of Tony Spilotro. Their targets included all the bookies, hustlers, pimps, and drug pushers who were not yet kicking up to the new self-declared boss of Las Vegas. Frank quickly got to work recruiting some guys. One of the first was Ernie Davino, an experienced thief with connections in New Jersey. Next was Leo Guardino, a Chicago native who also relocated to Vegas a while back. Guardino was trying to escape some heavy convictions and he was actually initially skeptical about Tony's Outfit connections, and only agreed after Cullotta assured him it had nothing to do with the Chicago bosses and that he wouldn't have to murder anyone. Wayne Matecki, another Chicago guy, was also recruited but he never permanently relocated; Frank kept him on a kind of retainer so he could fly out when there was a really big job or whenever someone needed to "disappear." Larry Neumann, a certifiably ruthless killer, was also recruited. Frank had met Neumann while he was in prison, and although he was recently paroled from what would have been a life sentence, he was already prepared to get back in the game. After Larry agreed to relocate, the core of the crew was solidified—Spilotro, Cullotta, Davino, Guardino, Neumann, and Matecki. The gang often had other guys working for them as associates, but they typically came and went, or were infrequent collaborators. For serious jobs, this core group of thieves were almost always involved. For years, Tony had kept a dominant grasp over the Las Vegas gambling scene with Lefty under his protection, all the while he was making a killing off his heist jobs. After his reunion with Frank Cullotta, he was ready to take the city by storm.

CHAPTER 6

HIGH TIMES AT THE STARDUST

Back in 1971, Lefty was still getting the lay of the land in Las Vegas. Tony had just arrived, and Lefty was just starting to become a big name in the city. Lefty was still a star handicapper and had one of the keenest eyes for sports in the game, but he was not yet infused into the fabric of Vegas' number one industry: the casinos. That time would come soon enough, but for now, his bookmaking sustained him. When he finally entered the casino business, it was a whole different story.

Time to Settle Down?

In 1971, Lefty Rosenthal was running a modestly sized (but not so modestly-named) betting office/bookie business that he called the Rose Bowl. As it turned out, the move from Illinois to Nevada didn't do a whole lot for his stress levels. His lifestyle in the desert was just as crazy and as busy as it was on the streets of Chicago or the beaches of Miami, and it was beginning to take its toll on his marriage with his new wife Geri. He was still laser-focused on studying and manipulating the odds of sports games, boxing matches, and the like. He was certainly successful enough to keep a woman like Geri happy, but he was not nearly as present as he could have been. Plus, the heat was starting to pick up in the 1970s. Without Tony present, Lefty was being harassed almost constantly and he was even arrested frequently, sometimes multiple times a month. Due to his inexhaustible luck he still always seemed to avoid incarceration, but it was a concerning situation, nonetheless.

Eventually, Geri got sick of the constant stress and her husband's obsession with gambling. She wanted him to quit and get out of the game for good. She wanted him to get a regular job and settle down for a while so that they could have a chance to be a real family. Surprisingly, Lefty agreed, albeit reluctantly. Lefty was a well-connected guy, and in Las Vegas, being well-connected meant you knew people who were higher-ups in the casinos. Lefty was easily able to get a job in the famous Stardust casino, a perfect place for someone like Lefty to take up a day job. He was originally hired simply as a floor manager, also known as a "pit boss." Basically, he was in charge of monitoring the gaming floor, which included surveilling both the players and the casino employees, with a particular focus on the blackjack tables. Blackjack was famous for being a favorite of cheats and card-counters, and it was one of the only casino games where the players could have an actual mathematical advantage over the house.

On Lefty's first day at Stardust, he had an unfortunate run-in with the blackjack manager, Frank Cursoli. Cursoli apparently just didn't like Lefty and had been giving him a hard time about taking a break because of his ulcer pain. It was the Vice President of Stardust, Bobby Stella, who stepped in and advised Cursoli to lay off of Lefty. Bobby was apparently pretty close with Lefty, and he told the blackjack manager that he simply didn't understand who Lefty was.

Cursoli protested, insisting that Lefty was no good, but Bobby seems to have convinced him to not get on Lefty's bad side. Still, Lefty wasn't having a good time. As he recalled, he wanted to quit on his very first day and go back to his high-rolling lifestyle, betting tens of thousands of dollars on a single game. It was Geri that convinced him otherwise. In another surprising sacrifice for the benefit of his young marriage, Lefty stuck it out.

By this point, Lefty was out of the bookmaking game, but he was still making his own personal bets, a process that required less of his attention and caused him less stress. Plus, it was what he was naturally best at. But he eventually started to put even his personal betting on the backburner. The first to go were the big, high roller bets that carried significantly more risk. Then he was betting less frequently. Soon his entire solo gambling career seemed to be put to an end. After a while, his only involvement in gambling was the occasional low stakes wager on a football game. He even gave up betting on horse races, the sport that he had grown up with and that had fostered his elite talent for analyzing the odds. With his hobby on pause for a while, most of Lefty's income was apparently coming from his perfectly honest and legitimate work monitoring the blackjack and craps tables at the Stardust.

Being as meticulous and detail oriented as Lefty was, he quickly picked up on just how crazy the concept of casinos actually was. For years, Lefty had done everything he could do to entice gamblers to take his bets and to make his odds more appealing to the takers. He learned how to manipulate both the numbers and the people to get everything to work to his advantage. But here in Las Vegas, people acted like they were frantic, even desperate to hand over their money to the house. And it wasn't just the big-time gamers that were dropping huge sums into the casino vaults. Without a second thought, a regular, average guy could end up losing 5, 10, even 20 thousand dollars at the tables, and more often than not, he would be back in no time to try to win it all back before inevitably losing thousands more. Lefty, of course, knew that people loved to gamble. What he hadn't yet realized was just how much folks were willing to throw away on a whim. Every day, people flew into Vegas from all over the country, even from around the world, on their own dime, just to donate their hard-earned money to the casinos along the Vegas Strip. Frankly, all of this amazed Lefty, and his obsessive focus on numbers, odds, and sports betting easily transferred into a fascination with casinos, their operation, and the psychology of the gamers. He no longer hated his job at the Stardust. He was on yet another mission to understand everything he possibly could about it.

"That's a Good-Looking Ten of Spades..."

Even when he was still back in Chicago, Lefty already knew the kind of opportunities a place like Las Vegas presented. But after spending some time within the casino world and seeing firsthand how they functioned, he realized that the Strip was a veritable haven for people like him, who had the knowledge and expertise to take advantage of people's financial irresponsibility. Along with that came the realization that, generally speaking, casinos were run sloppily and inefficiently. This was particularly true of the Stardust. Due to the fact that it was so easy to make money in running a casino, most of the people in charge barely even cared about it. The guys at the top only cared that piles of money were coming in, enough to make everyone happy, and they very rarely ever did anything to streamline or consolidate the operation of it. The floor managers were not exactly eagle-eyed, and they didn't particularly care to enforce the casino rules anyway. After all, lucky players and high rollers were sure to give them healthy tips, so why should they be sticklers? As much money as there was in the industry, there was so much more potential that had gone unrealized for years. Lefty saw it firsthand, and needless to say, he was intrigued.

While Lefty was still working as a pit boss, he started intensely patrolling the blackjack dealers that he was in charge of. He would analyze how they handled their cards and how they looked at them. He analyzed their mannerisms, whether they had certain tells, how they shuffled the deck and how they dealt their cards. He would often hang around behind the dealers and watch how they folded their cards up to look at them. He wanted to see if they were raising them too high and exposing them, making their table an easy target for card cheats working in pairs. Lefty wasn't exactly discrete about enforcing his rules either. In one instance, he noticed that one of his dealers was lifting his cards almost all the way off the table to look at them. Lefty approached the man and whispered to him, "that's a good-looking ten of spades you've got there!" (quoted in Pileggi, 1995). Lefty wasn't just keeping an eye on his own guys, though. Just as important was to monitor the players themselves.

One of the most important things Lefty learned in the early months of his casino career was that players would go to surprisingly great lengths to try and cheat the system that was essentially rigged in the casino's favor. Some of the tactics they developed were ingenious. One involved using teams of players that would sit at adjacent tables and watch the hands of the dealer at the other's table. These guys would prowl the casino floors looking for weak-handed dealers who exposed their cards too much and situate themselves in just the right way so that one of the players could easily peer over at the dealer's hand. Then, that player would signal to his partner what kind of hand his dealer had, using various techniques including hand gestures and morse code. Other techniques were much more advanced and creative. They included concealed devices that one partner would tap, sending radio signals to another device attached to the player making the bets. It was relatively easy to police the simpler methods, as most casinos eventually banned players from making hand gestures while at the table but hidden electronic morse code devices were much more difficult to detect. Either way, at the time, these casinos were mostly a free-for-all.

The methods could also be much cruder, too. One tried and true method involved a gang of co-conspirators that would create a distraction or diversion to draw the attention of other players, dealers, and security. The distraction could be a medical emergency, a fake jackpot celebration, or simply a bunch of guys acting rowdy. Regardless of method, while everyone was looking away from the tables, the partner making the bets would swap cards around, flip the dice before anyone could see the roll, or simply pocket as many chips as they could grab from the dealer's stack. While not exactly as refined as the other techniques, they were among the simplest ways to make a quick profit. There was also card counting, one of the favorite pastimes of blackjack pros and big-shot wannabes everywhere. This method was extremely difficult to detect and was, arguably, not even cheating per se. It involved keeping a mental tally of all the cards that have been dealt over the course of a game of blackjack and is used to determine whether the player or the dealer had the mathematical advantage during any given hand. For example, if the player was aware that most of the dealt cards were of low value, then most of the remaining cards in the deck would be high value. If the player's current hand was already in the high teens, they would be more than likely to bust if they accepted another card. This allowed the player to equalize the odds and take away the house's inherent advantage. It would be impossible to know for sure whether a given player was actually counting cards, and this made them the bane of casino managers everywhere. The solution was relatively simple, though. Casinos started using mixed decks for blackjack games, which were several decks merged together in order to make keeping track of the dealt cards far more difficult, if not impossible.

Even the slot machines, one of the casinos' most sure-fire moneymakers, were not safe from the cheaters that roamed the floors. Using special magnets that could manipulate the machinery within the slots, players were able to hit several jackpots in a row before disappearing. The odds of winning multiple consecutive jackpots were astronomical, and floor bosses would recognize immediately that the players were cheating, and so the players had to split fast or risk getting banned for life. Other players didn't require magnets and could actually break into the machines to rewire them, rigging them to increase their payouts and roll jackpots far more often. Since this involved physically opening the machines, these guys often worked in teams. Several of them would gather around the machine the player sat at, as if they were just watching his lucky streak. Meanwhile, the player would break into the machine behind the human wall. Some of these guys were so skilled that they required just a few seconds to get in, rewire it, and close it back up before anyone could catch a thing. For this reason, floor bosses were eventually placed on lookout for large crowds forming, and security cameras were often placed directly above the slots for a bird's eye view of the players, with security monitoring them incessantly. During Lefty's early years though, the Wild West was still very much alive in Las Vegas. He firmly believed that the casinos' inability to control these practices was a terrible waste.

Now, Lefty himself had claimed that during the time he was learning the tricks of the casino trade, he truly was just a floor manager, and nothing more. After all, he also claimed to have gone to Las Vegas as a freelancer of sorts, without official ties to the Chicago Outfit, so why would he have been anything other than a casino employee? Despite this, it didn't take long for people to notice that Lefty had a strange amount of influence for being just a floor guy. As time went on, people started to wonder exactly who he was. Even people outside the casinos started to notice something was off when Lefty began instituting policy changes at the Stardust, something that should have been above his paygrade. Slots were removed and placed with new ones, prices on drinks were changed, dealers replaced, even the food was meddled with, all apparently at the whim of Frank Rosenthal. He also clearly had the ear of Bobby Stella, the Stardust's VP, much to the chagrin of many senior executives at the casino resort. Lefty would talk, and Stella would listen, and whatever he wanted got done, or else heads would roll.

Unfortunately for Lefty, the rumors that the demanding floor boss from Chicago was more than he appeared to be did not escape the ears of the FBI. The feds, as well as local and state law enforcement, had been keeping tabs on Lefty since even before his arrival, and the idea that he was now plying his trade within a casino, possibly at the behest of gangsters from Illinois, was cause for concern. Vegas authorities began looking more closely at Lefty's professional life at the Stardust, and Nevada's Gaming Control Board chairmen began to wonder whether Lefty should be forced to acquire a "key employee" license. All higher-ups and executives within a casino, as well as anyone with significant influence, were required to hold these licenses in order to legally fulfill their job functions. The possession of these licenses was strictly enforced, and the granting of them was strictly regulated. Nobody deemed to be problematic or who had the potential to defraud the gaming industry was authorized to hold one of these key employee licenses, and because of Lefty Rosenthal's spotty track record of both proven and suspected gambling-related crimes, there was virtually no way that he was going to be able to get one. Lefty was well aware of this.

Lefty knew the Gaming Control Board was likely to demand that he apply for one of these licenses before too long, so he tried to circumnavigate their rules. He eventually abandoned his job as a pit boss and took a lower position in the casino, a position where it would be unrealistic to be required to hold a key employee license. Whatever new lowly title Lefty granted to himself, nothing much changed in his day to day. He still had the same routine, he still eyed down dealers and analyzed them for weaknesses, he still sent orders up the chain, and he still patrolled the floors of the Stardust, smoking his cigarettes and acting like he owned the place. People higher up the chain, like Alan Sachs, did not like the current state of affairs. Sachs was the President of the Stardust, and future owner of the Argent Corporation, the parent company of both the Stardust and Fremont casinos. Reportedly, he wanted Lefty gone from the casino floors as soon as the Gaming Control Board started sniffing around him. Like any sane casino operator, he wanted to avoid any undue attention from the Board, and clearly having a guy like Lefty around wasn't helping. Sachs probably would have had Lefty removed eventually, were it not for some of his associates, top guys in the Outfit, coming to visit Lefty one day and flexing their muscles around the Stardust. The Stardust President was aware of these men but hadn't aware that Lefty had such connections. After that, Sachs was suddenly quite happy to have Lefty around.

After this, Lefty's Outfit connections were essentially made public. Despite the fact that Lefty continued to insist he was a mere Stardust employee, everyone had the same assumption: he was sent there by the Chicago mob to take control of their casino interests. After the arrival of Tony Spilotro, most also assumed that he was sent there to be the muscle behind Lefty's brains and to ensure the Outfit's skim operation remained intact. This was despite the fact that Lefty insisted that Tony also arrived in Las Vegas as a "freelancer," like himself. Either way, Tony's arrival in Vegas certainly didn't help Lefty's situation. As soon as the Chicago enforcer arrived, the police began drawing the connection between the two. Lefty was working in a casino, and his old friend and wise guy was now there too, and they were associating with each other. Lefty had built a life for himself in Nevada, and he was transforming the Stardust into his own little empire, but with someone like Tony there to supposedly be in charge of his protection, he began to worry that everything might come crashing down.

In less than a year after Tony arrived in the Nevada desert, he was arrested. It was suspected that he was connected to a Chicago murder from back in the early 1960s, and just like what happened to Lefty when he was placed on a plane back to Chicago, Tony's tenure in Las Vegas was nearly finished before it truly got started. On the advice of Tony's legal defense team, he was going to need someone to testify to his character at his trial. He needed someone who had known him for a long time, and who would assure the jury the crime simply didn't fit Tony's moral character. He practically begged Lefty to do it. After all, Lefty was one of Tony's few friends or even acquaintances that didn't have an extensive rap sheet and who could reasonably pass as an upstanding citizen. Lefty was obviously very hesitant about the idea because it was a high profile case, and Lefty desperately wanted to stay out of the newspapers and the public attention. More importantly though, he didn't want any connections being made between himself and the Chicago Outfit. If the Gaming Control Board had any more reason to believe that he was crooked or in league with the Outfit, he may never see the inside of a casino ever again. Ultimately though, Lefty was a good friend and he wanted to help Tony. Of course, not doing so meant that he may run afoul of the Outfit, which he also desperately wanted to avoid. Regardless, Lefty provided an adequate character witness for Tony's trial. Tony was brought back to Chicago for his court proceedings, but he narrowly beat a conviction and wound up right back in the desert.

Not a Normal Man

In the mid-1970s, Allen Glick entered the picture. The big shot developer from California had wanted to get in on the Las Vegas casino scene for quite some time, but he needed a bit of help. As discussed in the previous chapter, that help came in the form of a substantial loan that was sourced from the Teamsters Union Pension Fund reserves. The loan was enough to bankroll the purchase of several casinos under his parent company, the Argent Corporation, as well as significant renovations and additions to the existing buildings. The loan, however, was conditional. It was acquired only with the help of Outfit ally Frank Balistrieri, who was also the notorious boss of the Milwaukee Crime Family. The Midwest Families, after all, had some of the strongest ties to corrupt labor unions. Balistrieri was also long suspected of being one of Lefty's associates.

After the deal was all said and done, Glick had his casinos and he probably felt like he was now the big man in charge. Unfortunately for Glick, Balistrieri was not nearly done with him. In fact, shortly after Glick received ownership of the Stardust, the Midwest boss had a favor to ask. Glick had to make things right with Lefty Rosenthal. Lefty was a man that was resented and held back by previous ownership, and he was now technically an employee of Glick's. Balistrieri told the Argent boss that Lefty, first and foremost, was a good guy. He told him that he was a spotless kind of character, and that he could be trusted in key decisions. He also told him that Lefty was the kind of guy that could end up making both Glick and him a ton of money. He told him Lefty was an important guy, and that he now had the duty to take care of him. It was heavily implied that Lefty should be receiving a hefty pay raise as well as more power within the casino as soon as possible. Indeed, Lefty's official annual salary was doubled in the years after Glick took over.

At first, Glick was hesitant at what he viewed as being an overstep. Why should some faraway businessman have any say in how he ran the casino or how he managed his staff? Balistrieri, of course, helped make it all possible, but Argent Corporation still belonged to Glick and the Stardust was still his property. When Glick pushed back even slightly, Balistrieri became enraged. Feeling threatened, Glick conceded and promised to meet with Lefty face-to-face to hash out the details of this new, coercive arrangement. Glick wondered who this Mr. Rosenthal was, and why Frank Balistrieri and his associates had such an interest in seeing him taken care of. So, he looked into him. Glick knew that Lefty was in the process of trying to acquire a gaming license, and that he did in fact have a bit of a spotty history with the law. He also knew of his organized crime associations. Glick did eventually meet up with Lefty, but he knew before he laid eyes on him that there was no way in hell Lefty was going to be able to get a license. That didn't matter though. He clearly had powerful friends.

After Lefty and Allen Glick had their meeting, it didn't take long for the Chicago floor boss to slowly but steadily start to take over operation of the Stardust. Lefty already had a lot of influence around the casino and especially the floor, but he had more power and support now than ever before. Lefty changed everything around to his liking. He hired and fired whoever he pleased, instituted strict rules for dealers and floor managers to follow, and renovated Glick's Stardust based on his own visions (later, he also furnished a large and beautiful office for himself). All of this, and more, he did without the permission or even awareness of Allen Glick. Lefty, being almost neurotically focused on the minutia, controlled even the most minor and particular details of the casino. In Martin Scorsese's film *Casino*, this is perfectly captured in a scene with Robert De Niro's character Sam "Ace" Rothstein, a portrayal of the real-life Lefty Rosenthal. Rothstein becomes irritated at the fact that his dining partner's muffin is filled with blueberries, while his muffin barely has any at all. He storms into the kitchen and institutes a new rule that demands the chefs count each and every blueberry going into the muffins, and ensure each one has the exact same amount. It would've probably tripled the time it took to make each muffin, but all Rothstein cared about was consistency and standards. Now, the film was partially fictionalized and dramatized, but it appears that there actually was truth to this story. Apparently, one of the rules the real Lefty Rosenthal enforced on the kitchens was that each muffin required exactly 10 blueberries, 10 chocolate chips, etc.

So, Lefty clearly had all the *real* power within the Stardust Casino and Hotel. Allen Glick, however, was still clinging to his delusions of being the top dog. Being the head of the Argent Corporation parent company should have granted him some special influence, but he found himself time and time again bending to the will of Lefty Rosenthal and his tough guy pals from Chicago and Milwaukee. Really though, Glick's delusions should have been shattered the second he laid eyes on the new office Lefty had renovated for himself. It was by far the biggest office in the entire casino, bigger than even Glick's himself. From behind those gilded doors, Lefty ran the day-to-day operations of the Stardust, while Glick tried in vain to assert some authority elsewhere. In reality, Lefty's glamorous new office was a terrible mistake. As always, he was meant to be keeping a low-profile. If Lefty had a gaming license and held a position of "official" power in the casino, the office would have been no big deal, but nobody in their right mind would have honestly believed that someone with Lefty's job title would have been given an office like that, nicer than the owner's. Still, he would soon be making even bolder moves. It was clear that, by 1974, Lefty was firmly in the process of seizing total control of the Stardust with the help and direction of his Outfit allies and connected business partners from out East.

Even worse for Glick, Lefty apparently was not simply going over his head or ignoring his orders. Lefty simply did not trust Allen Glick, something he realized before long. After a while, Glick started to get the feeling that he was being followed or being watched. He was right. He discovered that Lefty had actually hired some guys to tail Glick both within the casino and outside of it, and report back to Lefty on his movements and whereabouts. Glick, still defiantly unwilling to accept that there were powers at play that were even greater than himself, decided to retaliate, ordering his personal secretary to keep an eye on Lefty and report on what he was doing around the casino. It's unclear exactly what information Glick's secretary ended up sharing with him, but it likely included many things Lefty was doing behind his back that he didn't know about yet. Glick owned more than just the Stardust and he couldn't be in the casino all day, so having someone on the inside keeping tabs shed even more light on the extent of Lefty's influence in the building.

Eventually, Glick decided to confront Lefty about his behavior. He sat him down and interrogated him in regard to the men that had been following him around, and the liberty that he had taken in running the Stardust without Glick's knowledge. He also confronted Lefty about the myriads of times he had lied to Glick's face about what was going on within the casino. Glick had also learned that his own secretary was approached by Lefty who wanted her to keep tabs on Glick's activities while in the casino. He asked him about this too. When Lefty heard all of this, his face went red. He was normally a very calm man, but he had had enough of Allen Glick. Lefty stared Glick down, and his only response to the accusation that he had been spying on his boss was that he was going to fire Glick's assistant. Imagine this scenario. Lefty Rosenthal, an employee and subordinate of Allen Glick, had just threatened to fire Allen Glick's own secretary, all because she dared to expose his espionage. This was almost incomprehensible to Glick. Did he really just say that? Did he really just brush off the accusation of spying and hiring stalkers? He barely knew what to say. For the moment, he just stared blankly at Lefty, but years later he recalled what was going through his mind at the time: "That's when I realized I wasn't dealing with a normal man," (quoted in Pileggi, 1995).

CHAPTER 7

A SNAKE WITH TWO HEADS

Six years previously, Lefty Rosenthal had been little more than a fugitive on the run from federal agents who were bent on exposing his gambling crimes and his involvement with the Chicago mob. He had been forced out of Miami and was about to be forced out of his hometown for the second time. Fast forward to 1974, and he was sat down in a café, humiliating and intimidating the owner of the large Argent Corporation. He was dictating the course of business for a large casino on the famous Vegas Strip, and he had plenty of muscle, provided courtesy of Tony Spilotro, to back him up. His only obstacle to being in total control of the resort was Allen Glick. This obstacle was soon to be overcome for good.

For the Benefit of Others

When Glick had this most recent confrontation with Lefty, his fear finally set in. He was terrified and confused. He was still having trouble comprehending the fact that the deal he thought he made was, in fact, not the deal he got handed. He was about to find out the real terms of his arrangement with the Teamsters and their Midwest Mafia backers. When Glick finally collected himself enough to respond to Lefty's assertion that he would fire his assistant and continue to spy and keep tabs on Glick's movements, it wasn't what Lefty wanted to hear. He could not accept the way Lefty was talking and acting. He had long been concerned about the kind of power Lefty had over the rest of his employees, and this was apparently a step too far. Lefty, who was already frustrated at what he perceived as insubordination, was now thoroughly fed up. He was ready to simply walk away, but now these two needed to get a few things straightened out.

Lefty sat down with Glick and decided to calmly explain to him that, regardless of what title Glick held, what company he ran, where he was from, or who he knew, he simply *was not* Lefty's boss. He was not obligated to take orders from Glick, and he would not do so. He did not even have to consider his suggestions. He certainly did not have to call him "sir." In fact, as he explained to the Argent head, it was exactly the opposite. But Lefty couldn't just tell him that. He had to explain that he was not there, in the Stardust casino, for Glick's benefit, but rather "for the benefit of others," (quoted in Pileggi, 1995). He was not so naive as to drop the names of his connections, but Lefty was clearly referring to the Outfit and their allies in the Midwest. Glick already knew that the men who helped him secure his starting loans were sketchy at best, particularly Balistrieri, so it would not have taken much to draw this connection.

Still, Glick's dignity got in the way. Stunned, he tried to argue with Lefty. He wanted to push back against the man who was essentially threatening to take his casino and company away from him. Unfortunately for him, Lefty was not an easy man to push back against. He continued to explain to Glick that all of his protests and all of his complaints were for naught. They didn't matter. It was as if no one was speaking at all. Still, he insisted that Lefty take a back seat and stop meddling in the Stardust's affairs. Lefty had no choice remaining other than to flat out threaten his life. "If you interfere with any of the casino operations," Lefty told him as he held back his temper, "or try to undermine anything I want to do here, I represent to you that you will never leave this corporation alive," (quoted in Pileggi, 1995). With that, Glick calmed down. He didn't speak another word against Lefty to his face after that, and perhaps now he finally understood what kind of man he was dealing with.

Glick felt duped. There's no doubt that despite his willingness to climb into bed with dodgy characters, he was taken advantage of. It wasn't exactly a fair arrangement (or perhaps it was, considering Lefty and the Outfit allowed Glick to remain in his position while collecting a handsome salary), and Glick once again saw it fit to try to appeal to his original business contact who set up the deal with the Teamsters in the first place: Milwaukee crime boss Frank Balistrieri. He told Balistrieri what had happened and what Lefty had communicated. In response, Balistrieri kindly and politely told Glick to shut his mouth, deal with it, and that he had no choice in the matter. He had to listen to what Lefty said, because his word was law at the Stardust. One of Glick's other associates who assisted in the Argent-Teamsters deal was Nick Civella, who happened to also be a boss of the Kansas City crime Family. Civella, too, fully supported the Chicago bookmaker and told Glick that Lefty was going to be the one calling the shots in the future, not him. In reality though, both Balistrieri and Civella were based far away and didn't necessarily pose an immediate threat. They had a presence in the city, of course, but the real threat to Glick's safety was the iron in

Lefty's glove: Tony Spilotro. Spilotro would not need to be told twice if the order came down to "remove" Glick, and if Tony had his way, Glick probably would have already been beaten to a pulp by now for questioning Lefty's authority.

On paper, Allen R. Glick was a powerful man. At his peak in Las Vegas, he owned a whopping four casino resort locations, a number that was bested only by the notoriously reclusive Las Vegas billionaire business magnate Howard Hughes, who owned nearly twice as many locations. But, while Hughes was a man that was rarely seen in public and had little presence or regard on the street, Allen Glick was a well-known man that commanded respect in the public eye. He had been known for his honesty, modesty, and above all, his ethical business practices. A short while after he made his big move from Southern California to Nevada, he had come to be known as Las Vegas' "Golden Boy." He was a valued member of his community who was able to become massively successful, all with seemingly very clean business methods (although this last point obviously wasn't exactly true, Glick most probably would have preferred to maintain his clean business methods). He also happened to be a war hero. He was a decorated veteran of the Vietnam War who had been awarded the Bronze Star (granted for heroic acts during battle), the Medal of Honor (the United States Army's most prestigious award), and he had won Combat Air Medals on three separate occasions. Perhaps most of all, he was known simply as an upstanding, nice guy. He was a shining model of the virtues of Las Vegas, an ideal to strive toward.

This was the Allen Glick that the public saw. The Allen Glick behind the scenes, for much of the 1970s, was a different picture. He may have become massively successful, but in reality, he was merely a puppet whose strings were laid out across the country and were being pulled by faraway masters in Chicago, Kansas City, Milwaukee, and even Cleveland. He was not powerful in the traditional sense. At least in Las Vegas, his authority meant very little, even on his own property. He was still earning a ton of money, but all he had to do was keep quiet and acquiesce. Eventually, Glick accepted the fact that he would never be able to actually control his casinos, and that the real boss of the Stardust was Frank "Lefty" Rosenthal. Later, in October of 1974, Glick formally and publicly announced that Mr. Rosenthal would from now on be serving as his executive assistant in running the Stardust casino and hotel. It must have been a painful admission, but Glick still received all the benefits that came with being connected to vicious mobsters. In 1975, a connected guy named Marty Buccieri (who happened to be a relative of West Side boss Fifi Buccieri) came around trying to shake Glick down for around $30,000. Apparently, Marty believed that he was owed for whatever role he supposedly had behind the scenes in helping Glick secure the Teamsters cash, and he was now trying to extort him for more. Glick went to Lefty about the aggressive encounter, and within just a few days, Marty Buccieri was found dead with several gunshot wounds. Tony Spilotro, unsurprisingly, was always a prime suspect in the murder, but he never got charged for it.

Later on, Glick had a second run-in with yet another old friend and associate of his—Tamara Rand. Rand was a big-time investor who had a history of dealings with Glick. Apparently, she was involved to some extent in the Teamsters deal to acquire the Stardust and other casinos. Because of whatever role she had and her status as an investor in Argent, she believed she was entitled to a portion of the casinos as well. Glick, however, denied that she deserved any kind of controlling portion of the company, much to the frustration of Rand. It's unclear exactly how much Rand had to do with Glick's casino acquisitions, but in response to his rebuttal, she threatened to sue both Glick personally, as well as his company, the Argent Corporation (which, at least on paper, owned the Stardust, the Hacienda, and the Fremont).

Again, Glick turned to none other than Lefty, who happened to be just about the only guy Glick could turn to anymore. Lefty then reported this news to his bosses. After all, a lawsuit against the company would surely invite unwanted attention and it would inevitably involve some close scrutiny of the true ownership of Argent Corporation's casinos. This could have exposed a paper trail leading all the way back to Frank Balistrieri, Nick Civella, and Joe J. Aiuppa, the current head of the Chicago Outfit. Aside from that risk, the true controllers of Argent didn't appreciate the idea of anyone else laying claim to a portion of their profit. Just like what happened with Marty Buccieri, within just a few days of the confrontation with Glick, Tamara Rand was found dead, and again, everyone assumed Tony was behind it. With these annoyances out of the way, Lefty and Glick continued to expand operations. Later in 1975, they acquired their fourth casino, the Marina hotel resort.

The Great Innovator

Few people realize how much of Las Vegas' current and historical practices can be attributed to Lefty Rosenthal. It was actually quite remarkable how much he was able to accomplish when he had free reign. Glick was certainly an impediment early on, and even after

Lefty's half threats, Glick continued to try to "muscle" him out. This was usually by subversive methods like simply reversing the changes Lefty had made without his consent and by holding large, important meetings without Lefty's presence or knowledge. Once Glick was put in his place and made to realize exactly what kind of role he and Lefty were each expected to have, the dynamic changed entirely. With seemingly all the power a man could have in a city like this, and without having to worry about Glick meddling in his affairs, Lefty was free to revolutionize the Stardust, the casino industry, and the city of Las Vegas as a whole. Across all of Argent's casinos, Lefty's presence was felt, but his base of operations was always the Stardust.

In 1976, Lefty instituted one of the most significant of these innovations. It came through the merging of two of his passions: sports betting and casino operations. Sports betting had long been looked down upon by the more senior, traditional Las Vegas casino moguls. It was considered an "unglamorous" breed of gambling that evoked images of rowdy sports fans, beer spilling out of mugs onto the floor, and a general lower-class vibe that was unfit for their ritzy resorts. They preferred the bright, flashing lights of the slot machines and the quiet dignity of their blackjack dealers. It was also simply seen as a worse way to make money compared to table games and slots. It wasn't as reliably profitable, and the possibility of outside influences (for example, people like Lefty bribing players to throw games) interfering with the odds took away some of the house's innate advantage. Even horse racing, the "sport of kings," wasn't a common betting medium at the time.

Lefty, a street kid from Chicago's West Side, was not quite so pretentious as his Vegas counterparts, so the "low class" status that sports betting had was not much of a bother to him. He also knew better than anyone in perhaps the entire country just how profitable sports betting could actually be, both for the player who understood the game and for the one offering the odds. He saw through all of the reservations, and he wanted to bring his favorite pastime to the Vegas Strip. To that end, he opened up the city's first ever sports and horse racing betting parlor, which was located right inside the Stardust. It was a beautiful and modern theatre space and was equipped with a luxurious lounge for the players and viewers. It was filled with huge televisions mounted on the walls that were constantly playing games from every American sport imaginable, plus horse races from around the country. Not only could players go there to place their wagers, but they could stay, relax in luxury, and watch the same games they just bet on while having some drinks. This meant they would stay in the casino for longer, encouraging them to spend even more cash.

Lefty's sportsbook parlor became very successful in a short period of time, being one of the few nice places in town that offered such a service. Before long, those same old school Vegas guys that looked down upon Lefty's favorite hobby were now clamoring to try and copy his success. Suddenly, this same style of parlor became a staple in almost every single casino in Las Vegas, and they remain popular today. This revolution may have seemed obvious, but it was a huge game changer for the city, Lefty, and the mobsters that he represented. Not all of his changes were so grand, though. Others were far more subtle, like when he broke the tradition of all-male card dealers and began hiring young women to fill these roles.

Female blackjack dealers were almost unheard of in Vegas (and around the country) prior to Lefty's arrival, but Lefty understood the minds of gamblers, especially the chronic ones and the high rollers, more than anyone around. He knew that a big part of gambling, for many, was image. Big bets were impressive. Doubling down was ballsy. And when they won the bet, they also won the admiration (or jealousy) of everyone else at the table. When women were around, the drive to impress was even greater. The only way to guarantee there were ladies around was to have them be the ones dealing the cards. A lot of the high rollers Lefty knew often had so much pride and ego that they would make unusually large bets just to impress spectators, and the idea of giving up after a loss was embarrassing. Lefty knew that if he staffed his tables with attractive young women, not only would players be more drawn to them and stay at them longer once there, but they were also far less likely to walk away after a defeat. This proved to be a surprisingly effective little tactic, and sure enough, it helped to nearly double the Stardust's income from blackjack in under 12 months.

Aside from these strategic implementations, Lefty was also fiercely and ruthlessly protective over the Stardust and its cashflow. Even the smallest of cheaters was unacceptable and was dealt with harshly. There is a story, now made infamous by its portrayal in Scorsese's *Casino*, of an instance when Lefty was personally patrolling the floor and observing the blackjack tables as he had done when he first began working at the Stardust. Despite being the top shot-caller at the casino, Lefty still preferred to do his own dirty work and monitor everything himself. On this day, he managed to discover a pair of cheaters working in tandem at separate, adjacent tables. The dealer at the first player's table was making a fatal error:

lifting his cards too high to look at them, exposing them to players behind him. The other partner at the next table had a clear line of sight to the other dealer's hand and had been sending signals to the first partner, revealing the dealer's cards. Guys like these were common, and the scheme they were running was typical along the Strip. They would stroll around the floor and observe some of the tables, looking for weak-handed dealers and then situating themselves appropriately to be able to carry out their operation.

When Lefty felt he had enough evidence that they were cheating, he didn't pull any punches. He had a member of his security team walk up behind one of the players and secretly stun him with a kind of cattle prod device he had concealed in his jacket. The shock simulated severe cardiac arrest, and Stardust security quickly rushed to "help" him. They picked him up and said they were taking him to receive medical attention, but in reality, they dragged him into the Stardust's backroom to interrogate him: "We ripped his trousers and found the electronic device he was using to receive the signals. That was proof enough for me," (Pileggi, 1995). Lefty noticed that the player had been using his right hand as his dominant hand when handling his cards. He saw it as an appropriate punishment to make him a lefty instead. On his orders, Lefty's security team held the cheater down while another smashed his right hand with a rubber mallet, shattering the bones in the fingers. Instead of killing him, they gave him a warning. If he ever showed his face at any of the casinos that Lefty claimed as his own, including the Stardust, the Hacienda, the Marina, and the Fremont, he would never walk out again.

With all of this, the operation of the four Outfit-backed casinos became far more efficient and profitable. The Outfit's skim operation was going on smoothly due to Lefty's managerial oversight and the brute protection of Tony "the Ant" Spilotro, and Chicago's presence in Nevada was growing considerably. All the right people (i.e., the Midwest bosses back home) were happy. The legitimate profits of the Stardust and the other Rosenthal-controlled resorts were skyrocketing, and without a doubt, Lefty was the man responsible for that. Lefty always received preferential treatment from the mob despite not being eligible for actual membership, but now, he had made himself truly indispensable.

CHAPTER 8

THE ROSENTHAL SHOW

In the latter half of the 1970s, the Stardust was thriving, as were Lefty and Tony. Glick was now firmly in on the scheme and served dutifully as the Outfit's front man who would divert attention away from the shadowy mob figures in the background. For a while, it seemed like the entire world revolved around Lefty and his casinos. Operations were running smoothly, millions of dollars in cash were being skimmed from casino profits and sent out West to the bosses, and Lefty had Tony at his side ensuring that nobody messed with either himself or the Outfit's operation. Unfortunately, an old thorn in Lefty's side continued to pester him into these years. That was the Nevada Gaming Commission and their desire to get Lefty as far away from the inside of a casino as possible. Lefty would never accept the fact that the Commission could push him out entirely, and the more restrictions they tried to place on him, the more his ego grew in response. After a while, the Stardust had turned into the Rosenthal Show. It was all about him, and that proved to be bad for business.

Getting Famous

As the booming 1970s chugged along, things started taking a turn for the worse. It was not yet catastrophic, but the gaze of the Gaming Commission was getting stronger all the time. Then in 1976, the Nevada gambling authorities determined amongst themselves that, despite whatever titles he had, Lefty truly was the man behind the curtain. They no longer had any reason to doubt that reality and given the fact that he was at the Stardust, clearly making key decisions while not in possession of a gaming or "key employee" license, this was a major cause for concern. Shortly after, the Commission placed new, severe restrictions on Lefty and what he was able to do within the four Argent casinos, including Stardust. As a direct result of these restrictions, Lefty was no longer able to serve as Glick's "executive assistant" in any official capacity. For a while, Lefty had been exploiting a loophole that allowed anyone to participate in the management of a casino's structure, so long as they were currently in the process of applying for a license. Knowing that Lefty wouldn't get approved, his Mafia connections and advisors encouraged him to continue switching his job title, so that his application would constantly be put at the bottom of the list without ever having to actually receive a decision on his application. Now, the Commission had ended this little scam.

Back in 1974 when Lefty first applied for his license, he was denied it almost instantly on the basis of his gambling history, reputation, and association with the Outfit in general and Tony Spilotro in particular. Lefty was enraged, but later with the help of crooked lawyer and future Las Vegas mayor Oscar Goodman, he decided to appeal and successfully had the decision overturned, as it was determined that the panel did not give him a fair assessment and that their judgement was premature. This was a win, at least for a short time. But, not too long afterwards, the Nevada Supreme Court decided to step in, and they were adamant that Frank Rosenthal would not receive a key employee license under any circumstances. Shortly after this, they actually passed legislation that stated that no person who had been deemed "unqualified" to receive such a license was now able to hold *any position* within a casino or gambling establishment, nor could they even associate with qualified casino operators. This meant that the very fact that Lefty applied in the first place had potentially doomed his career on the Strip. That is, it would have if not for yet another built-in loophole.

Although the Supreme Court's decision was highly restrictive and rigid, there was one sector of casino operations that were exempt from these conditions. That was casino entertainment. Everyone from the directors to the event planners to the entertainment talent themselves were to be free from scrutiny under the Gaming Commission and the state licensing laws, and it was all because of one man: Frank Sinatra, the world-famous singer and arguably the most popular performer in the history of the Las Vegas Strip. Frank Sinatra was already a legend in the entertainment business by the 1970s. His career kicked off in the mid-1930s and carried a singing legacy that spanned over five decades. He had a silky-smooth baritone voice that drew crowds from all over, and he became a staple in the Las Vegas scene by the 1950s. He also happened to be notoriously well-connected to the Mafia. Nevada officials knew full well the kind of associates Mr. Sinatra had, and they knew that someone like him should have been disallowed from entering casinos under the new strict regulations. But that was too jagged a pill to swallow. They didn't want to have to ban one of the city's biggest draws, plus they knew that there were plenty of other Vegas entertainers who had some shady friends, including Tony Bennett (a known associate of New York City's Bonanno Family), and even Mr. Las Vegas himself, Wayne Newton, who was long suspected of being a close friend of the Gambino Family, but he personally denied this. Because of this, anyone involved in the entertainment side of casino management had little to fear from the bureaucrats and enforcers at the Gaming Commission as well as their new legislation. This presented a glaring opportunity.

The opportunity wasn't lost on Lefty. He was facing permanent removal and a lifetime ban from stepping foot into his casino, so it didn't take much consideration to change his title yet again. At the snap of his fingers, he became the Stardust's brand-new Entertainment Director. This was a role that, on paper, should have had absolutely nothing to do with key casino decisions nor operating the management structure in any way. His sole responsibility should have merely been to provide entertainment for guests, which was firmly outside the realm of gambling. In reality though, Lefty could continue with his regular day-to-day activities, because by simply placing himself in this role he didn't have to worry about the licensing troubles. Lefty could have been a custodian for all he cared, so long as he was able to maintain his grasp over Glick. Still, in an effort to at least give the appearance that he was fulfilling his official job duties, Lefty immersed himself in the entertainment side of the Stardust. Of course, Lefty wasn't much of a singer, and he certainly didn't have the skill set to be a major stage performer. He did prove, however, that he was more than willing to put himself in front of a camera and a live audience.

Perhaps to prove his new role to everyone (or, perhaps, because he just wanted the spotlight), Lefty debuted *The Frank Rosenthal Show* in 1977 with himself as the star host. It was billed as a kind of variety show that would be filmed in front of an audience right on the Stardust casino floor. Given Lefty's extensive connections, he had no problem attracting huge, headlining guests. Ironically, one of his first ever guests happened to be Frank Sinatra. Other world-famous guests included star athletes like Yankees 2nd baseman Billy Martin, Cleveland Browns legend Jim Brown, baseball Hall of Famer Tommy Lasarda, and the now-highly controversial football star O.J. Simpson. Also appearing were the flashy and eccentric pianist Liberace (dubbed the "King of Bling" due to his extensive jewelry collection), and even legendary comedian Don Rickles. Funny enough, Don Rickles later went on to play the role of Sam Rothstein's (the fictional Lefty) casino manager, Billy Sherbert, in Scorsese's *Casino*.

The Frank Rosenthal Show was slated to air on Saturday evenings, but for the first part of its existence, it had an irregular and erratic schedule which affected its popularity. Sometimes they would skip a week and there wouldn't even be an announcement. Fans would tune in only to have some other program come on instead. It seemed that Lefty would just do an episode whenever he managed to get a good guest to come on, and airing times varied wildly until they finally got a solid audience and steady stream of celebrity guests. Even when the Stardust managed to get their schedule figured out, the show was widely panned and generally regarded as poor quality. There was never really a clear point to the show, and sometimes guest interviews would be interrupted by random events going on at the Stardust. Lefty clearly wasn't a gifted people-person, and that came through in his interactions with people like Sinatra. Yet somehow, it still attracted a ton of viewers when they filmed, even if they were fans who just wanted to witness the spectacle or listen to their favorite celebrities respond to uninteresting or irrelevant questions from Mr. Rosenthal. As a result, the recognition of Lefty's name went through the roof. He went from being an unassuming and relatively unknown casino employee to being one of the most easily recognizable faces on the Las Vegas Strip. People would stop and stare when he went out in public, fancy restaurants would jump to secure him the best seats in the house, and he even began travelling with an entourage. For Lefty's mobster friends, many of whom were to thank for his career in Vegas in the first place, this was a nightmare.

The Dry Snitch

The new show was definitely a boost for Lefty's popularity, but it had a noticeable effect on his personality as well. Most of his friends, including Tony Spilotro, believed it had turned him into a self-centered egomaniac. He was always a snappy dresser, but he had started wearing the flashiest clothing he could find and had reportedly expanded his wardrobe to encompass literally hundreds of different outfits. He wore expensive, oversized sunglasses and only smoked his cigarettes through long, elegant cigarette holders. It was sometimes so over the top that he resembled the caricature of a rich man. He dressed more like an eccentric celebrity than a guy who was supposed to be keeping a low profile. Now, if Lefty was in the room, it was almost impossible not to notice him, and his mob friends wondered if that was his goal all along.

The bosses back in Chicago, Kansas City, and Milwaukee hated that Lefty was turning himself into a public figure, and the fact that he was now on television was deeply embarrassing and a major thorn in their side. They obviously did not want the face of a guy who had known connections to the Midwest Families to be plastered all over the city, and they certainly didn't want his name (or any of theirs) to start appearing in the media. Tony resented it as well. He was in the process of building something that would have truly been his own out in Nevada, and the one thing that threatened to destroy all of it was the bosses turning on him. The only way to prevent that was to ensure that the skim taking place at Lefty's casinos remained profitable. It was his only real task while he was out there, and if he failed, it would have been game over for him, Cullotta, and the entire Hole in the Wall Gang. Lefty, now more than ever, was putting that in serious jeopardy by bringing ever more unwanted attention to himself and the operation of the Stardust.

To make matters worse, everyone immediately realized that *The Frank Rosenthal Show* was a completely self-serving vanity project. Lefty was using it mostly as a platform to start a heated, public feud between himself, the Nevada Gaming Commission, and the Gaming Control Board. On an almost weekly basis, Lefty stood in front of his national audience and attacked both the Commission and its member chairmen, claiming that they were dirty, crooked, incompetent, or that they had some kind of prejudicial vendetta against him for his past (which he claimed they exaggerated). Lefty clearly refused to accept the fact that the Commission would never give him a license, allowing him to legitimately run his establishments, and decided that he needed a public forum if he wanted to win. But for the bosses, this was a disaster. Things were running fine as they were, and even though some gymnastics were required to keep Lefty in the casinos, they were still collecting their stacks of cash. When Lefty started appearing on TV and calling out Commission chairmen by name, they genuinely wondered if he may have had a mental breakdown.

Lefty even got several of his guests to participate in the denigration of the gambling authorities. They would agree with whatever Lefty said during his rants and go further to suggest that entities like the Gaming Commission were ruining the great experiment of Las Vegas. The city was supposed to be a haven for free-spirited gamblers and gamers, free from the pompousness and the strictures of the rest of the country. Vegas was supposed to be synonymous with freedom. Now, they argued, it was being turned into some kind of authoritarian dictatorship run by the Commission chairmen. They had apparently abused their political power and were trying to seize the city and the casinos for themselves. These statements were obvious exaggerations, but it was clear that Lefty was waging a public relations war against the men preventing him from acquiring a license. He also had no issue calling out several of the men responsible by name. One of these people was Chairman Henry Reid. Reid was an important man with a lot of friends, and he would later go on to serve in the Senate. Lefty still chose to personally attack him on his program. As if all this weren't bad enough, Lefty even started writing columns and opinion pieces for Las Vegas Sun newspaper, exposing his name, his connections, and his wild opinions even more. Antics like these were becoming a serious problem.

The Outfit leadership as a whole as well as Tony tried to convince Lefty to stop. By calling out important political figures by name, he was inviting so many unwanted eyes to their operation. Perhaps Lefty was becoming unstable. Who knew what he would say next? He started discussing things that he should not have been discussing and people from all over the city were tuning in each week to hear his words. Among some Vegas and Midwest gangsters, Lefty started to get a reputation as a "dry snitch." These were people who did not actually snitch by running to the cops and blabbing, but instead they would reveal sensitive information publicly that could do damage to the Family or its business. Whether it was intentional or simply due to incompetence, "dry snitching" was often as much justification for having someone "taken out" as actually talking to the police was. For the time, Lefty was still an important guy and he had more than his share of friends in high places, so his life was not in danger. Still, if anything started to seriously impact the skim, life would start to change very quickly for both Lefty and Tony.

On top of all of this, the Outfit bosses were well aware that Lefty's new role as Entertainment Director wasn't fooling anyone, especially the Las Vegas authorities who were still convinced Lefty was behind everything. His position was not meant to be a permanent solution and the fact that they could expect continued harassment as long as Lefty was unlicensed meant that sooner or later, something would have to give. Either Lefty would need to receive the official blessing of the Commission, or he might have to take a step back. Lefty's continued hostile attitude toward the men responsible for certifying him made the first possibility less and less likely with each episode of *The Frank Rosenthal Show* that aired.

Therefore, TV show or no TV show, one of Lefty's top priorities given to him by the bosses was still acquiring a gaming license to operate the Stardust, something that they knew had been a virtual impossibility since before he even arrived in the city.

The growing concerns about Lefty and his ability to continue soundly running the Stardust emanated outward into the casinos run by the other Families as well. It was correctly believed that any legal shenanigans that might affect the Outfit would inevitably damage others as well. Joe Agosto was just one of the many mob operators in Las Vegas that was scared to death of what Lefty might do. Agosto was in Las Vegas as a representative of the Civella Crime Family of Kansas City, and he was heavily involved in the Tropicana casino hotel (the same establishment where Lefty met his wife, Geri). Under different circumstances, Agosto and Lefty would have been in much the same boat. Agosto too was unable to secure a key employee license and had also taken up the role of Entertainment Director, the same title Lefty held at the Stardust, to wiggle his way around the law. Unlike Lefty however, he did not decide to air his dirty laundry in front of the entire city. He saw what his counterpart at the Stardust was doing, and he knew it was going to mean trouble for him and his bosses as well. He frequently called the guys back home in Kansas City to complain about all the attention he was receiving. He told them that Lefty was a guy who just didn't know how to keep his mouth shut. He told them what he was doing was dangerous. Finally, he told them that, in his opinion, Lefty and his ever-growing ego were going to bring the whole operation crashing down, not just for the Stardust and the Chicago Outfit, but for every single mob-connected racket in the city. Only time would tell if Agosto was right to worry.

CHAPTER 9

CRASHING DOWN

So, in the late 1970s and going into the early 1980s, the antics of both Lefty and Tony had started to catch up with them. Lefty had made a celebrity out of himself and painted a huge target on the backs of himself and his associates. Tony's spree of violence that had brought so many of the criminal rackets in the city under his heels had also brought a ton of heat down on Las Vegas, a city that the mob had been trying to keep clean and orderly for decades. The pair of Chicago kids had been handed everything they could have asked for on a silver platter. It was one that promised a life of easy living, luxury, and power. Lefty and Tony each had their own special set of flaws, and in the end, they both helped to ruin everything. Within a few years, all they had built, from their businesses to their personal relationships, was threatening to come crashing down on their heads.

Tony, Frank, and Geri

Around the same time that *The Frank Rosenthal Show* was picking up major steam on television and around the city, Lefty's personal relationships were starting to crumble. Lefty and Tony had already grown bitter toward each other, which actually started years ago when Lefty was hesitant about Tony moving to Vegas permanently. Lefty blamed Tony for bringing so much heat to the city (indeed, since Tony and Frank Cullotta's Hole in the Wall Gang began operating in the city, the rate of murder and violent crimes had skyrocketed) and for putting his good name in jeopardy. Whenever Tony or his gang made headlines, Lefty was invariably mentioned due to their years-long history dating back to their time in Chicago. It had become exceedingly difficult to run a "clean" operation this way, and he fully blamed Tony for this. He also believed that, above everything else, Tony was the number one reason that Lefty was never able to acquire a gaming license. Putting aside Lefty's own, personal history with gambling related crimes, he thought that if Tony had never relocated to Nevada, the Gaming Commission chairmen would not have given him nearly as hard of a time. Apparently, Tony was the one they were *actually* worried about.

At the same time, Tony blamed Lefty for garnering so much of the public's attention via *The Frank Rosenthal Show*. The Outfit's top brass had clearly articulated their displeasure with the situation in the Stardust, and Tony believed that Lefty was not acting like the subordinate that he was. Lefty had plenty of people above him who called the shots, but he had lost sight of all of that, and Tony was more and more seeing him as a guy not worth his protection. It didn't help that Tony envisioned himself as the true boss of Las Vegas who was only nominally tied to the Chicago Outfit, while in reality operating his own distinct fiefdom where everyone paid tribute to him. He believed that Lefty's new big shot attitude was out of place. Lefty had gotten too big for his own good, and no longer respected Tony's position. In his mind, he was the only reason that Lefty was allowed to operate the Argent casinos in the first place.

Without him, Lefty Rosenthal was just another guy to take advantage of. Tony even claimed to his friends that Lefty had started to ignore him in public. When Lefty would enter a restaurant with his pretentious entourage of followers, he wouldn't even acknowledge Tony if he was there with his associates. Tony got the feeling that Lefty was pretending he didn't even exist, which greatly devalued their friendship. Since the day he arrived in Las Vegas, Tony wanted to be the big man in town, and to a degree, he resented Lefty's celebrity status. Lefty, on the other hand, simply thought Tony was jealous of his new public persona.

Despite the fact that their protective relationship was breaking down, Lefty couldn't escape his constant public association with Tony. They could have hated each other, but the media would still mention Lefty by name as one of Tony's connections whenever the Outfit enforcer made headlines. By the early 1980s, this was haunting Lefty. Both the FBI and Nevada officials were finally making headway in their crackdown against the violent crime spree of the Hole in the Wall Gang. Back in 1978, the feds secured one of their biggest scores against Tony's crew by successfully bugging his jewelry store, the Gold Rush. Tony, Cullotta, Blitzstein, and their associates had used the Gold Rush as the headquarters of a large fencing operation for years, so extensive wiretaps were almost certain to divulge something of interest. Indeed, they did. Over the several months during which state and federal law enforcement were actively surveilling Tony's shop, they heard enough incriminating conversations to justify a massive raid targeting Tony and his properties. In both Las Vegas and Chicago, teams of dozens of federal agents simultaneously stormed various locations connected to Tony and seized everything they could, from files to physical cash.

The raid was highly publicized in Nevada and Illinois, and it was very big news in the criminal underworld. Even though it had nothing to do with Lefty, "Frank Rosenthal" was still mentioned alongside Tony in almost every publication. Still, from the mid-to-late 1970s, Tony's crew continued protecting Lefty and his casinos. Around this time, Frank Cullotta had discovered a pair of blackjack cheats working together to scam the Stardust. One of them actually turned out to be an Outfit guy named Joey DiFronzo. When Tony was informed of what was going on, he ordered DiFronzo to evacuate the city permanently, and he threatened to rat him out to the bosses back home if he refused. The end of this long-standing arrangement, however, was clearly in dire straits by the end of the decade. Without Tony's protection, there was a very real question as to whether or not Lefty's safety could be guaranteed. Everyone in town would want a piece of his business, and besides that, he had made his fair share of enemies. Many of them were former friends.

Perhaps unsurprisingly, Lefty and Tony's relationship wasn't the only one faltering. Around the same time, Lefty was also in the middle of a falling out between himself and his wife, Geri. You didn't have to know Geri all that well to guess that she wouldn't exactly be satisfied with a quiet, married life. She was used to patrolling the city of Vegas at night, touring all the flashiest casinos hunting for her prey. For the past few years, however, she was expected to act as an accessory to Lefty, her big-time casino executive husband who never had enough time to give her. Even after Geri was finally able to convince Lefty to give up his hectic and high-stress gambling lifestyle, it wasn't very long at all before he was back in the game. By the late 1970s, Geri was completely discontent, and what had once been a casual relationship with drugs and alcohol became a crippling addiction.

Lefty and Geri ended up having two children together, but Geri proved she was not up to the task of being a mother. Geri was cold toward her children, and she resented the fact that they had become Lefty's top priority. Lefty adored his kids, and although Geri hadn't felt like she was the center of his attention since the two got married, her feelings of being an afterthought got much worse after she saw how Lefty fawned over the babies. She wondered why he didn't treat her the same way or look at her with the same love he had for the kids, but perhaps it was because Lefty always knew deep down that Geri didn't love him. Unable to bear the life she had built for herself with him, Geri would often disappear without warning, sometimes staying away for days before returning home to Lefty, who began accusing her of cheating on him with Lenny Marmor or one of the myriad romantic interests she had started in Vegas since she arrived there from California (there were indeed several occasions that Geri went home to visit Marmor, the father of her first child). Even when Geri was home, as far as her kids were concerned, she may as well have been away. Her ever-deepening drug abuse problems often rendered her unable to care for her children, so that responsibility was placed at Lefty's feet as well.

Geri's secretiveness about where she went all the time was the main reason for Lefty's suspicion that she was being unfaithful to him. Although he had accepted years ago that he would never be the man Geri wanted, he was absolutely unwilling to share her or let her go.

For better or for worse, she was his. Sometime earlier, Lefty had discovered that Geri had begun hanging out again with an old fling of hers from back at the Tropicana named Johnny Hicks. Lefty actually got into a physical altercation with Hicks over Geri years ago at Bugsy Siegel's old Flamingo Casino and Hotel back in 1969. The fact that they were speaking again, possibly even seeing each other romantically, was intolerable. Coincidentally, Hicks was shortly afterward found shot to death outside of his apartment, just a few days after Lefty reportedly accused Geri of having an affair with him. This was very likely the handiwork of one of Tony Spilotro's crew, who Lefty often used as a cudgel to get what he wanted. Obviously, Geri knew full well what kind of man Lefty was and what kind of friends he had, and she automatically blamed Lefty for his death. She felt trapped, like she wasn't allowed to be the kind of person she used to be. She was flirty, and she was sentimental, but Lefty allowed room for none of that. Geri, due to a combination of narcotics, alcohol, and awe-stricken grief, flew off the handle and stormed out of their home.

It wasn't at all uncommon, especially in the late 1970s, for Lefty and Geri to get in physical fights. Geri was undoubtedly unstable at this point, and she was known to be violent on occasion. Lefty, seeing himself as the one responsible for granting his ungrateful wife a life of prosperity and extravagance, usually responded in kind. On one occasion, Lefty and Geri got into a particularly violent fight, and by the end of it, both of them were injured and Geri had decided to take her children while Lefty was gone and run away with them to go to Lenny Marmor. Together, the pair and the three children took off. Lefty was in constant contact with her and pleaded for her to at least let him come pick up the children. After that, he didn't care what she did. She could disappear forever with her scumbag Southern California boyfriend, as long as he had his two kids. Before long, however, in true Geri McGee fashion, Geri and Lenny ran out of money (likely blowing it all on cocaine and pills) and she was forced to return to him, penniless. Lefty had used all the resources at his disposal, including some of Tony's guys, to track her down, but it was desperation that ultimately brought her back. Even though she was back home, she had very nearly stolen Lefty's children away for good, and there was no coming back from this. Their relationship was effectively over.

So, both Tony and Geri, arguably two of the people closest to Lefty in his life, were drifting away from him. Further complicating this was that while this was happening, the two were also drifting closer to each other. Geri and Tony's wife Nancy had been close friends for years and would often hang out with each other whenever Tony and Lefty got together to discuss business. But it was Tony that had her husband's ear, so Geri often sought the counsel of Tony when she needed advice on how to deal with Lefty and his behavior. Sometimes she just needed someone that she could complain to, and seeing as though Tony was also frequently upset with the Stardust executive, it worked out perfectly for both of them. Apparently, this confidant-style relationship sparked a romance between them, because at some point, Geri had begun cheating on Lefty with Tony. They bonded over their anger toward him and helped fuel each other's belief that he was actually going crazy and putting everything they had built for themselves in jeopardy. They were driven into each other's arms, and although they both knew it was a huge mistake, they continued the affair for quite some time behind Lefty's back and it would later bring severe consequences for both of them. In Lefty's world though, this wasn't nearly his only concern. All the while his public feud with the Gaming Commission continued, and the breakdown of his personal relationships were only some of the tragedies that the late 1970s brought.

Glick's Downfall

Allen R. Glick, the property investor and Argent Corporation operator from San Diego, was undoubtedly a key piece in the Outfit's Vegas operations, at least as far as the Stardust, Hacienda, Marina, and Fremont casino resorts were concerned. Despite all of Lefty's talk and his threats against Glick, the man's name carried value. Unfortunately for him, he was valuable only insofar as his reputation remained spotless. By the mid-to-late 1970s, his luck in this regard was already starting to take a turn for the worse. In 1976, Nevada authorities discovered that Glick had in fact used portions of the loan money he secured from the Teamsters toward his own personal expenses, which included paying off some of his personal debts. If true, this essentially amounted to embezzlement of company funds on the part of the Argent Corporation. For a casino that was operated by vicious Chicago mobsters, the last thing they needed was for their front man to also be seen as a dishonest criminal, especially a guy like Glick who for so long was one of the city's most highly respected businessmen.

Glick was implicated in 1976 when Nevada authorities actually raided some of the casinos, including the Stardust. They already suspected there may have been significant income being siphoned out of the casino stores, and indeed, they discovered a large slot machine skimming operation that over the years had extracted millions out of the Stardust's slot income. Glick wasn't brought down by this, but it was one of the earliest signs of his corroding reputation. Suspected financial crimes weren't the only things that were sticking to Glick. He was also heavily implicated in more than one homicide. The suspicious gangland style murders of both Marty Buccieri and especially Tamara Rand raised many eyebrows in Glick's direction. Both of the victims were known to have been either current or former associates of Glick, and both of them had reason to be displeased with him, given the Argent Corporation's shadowy financial history. Plus, there was a clear trail leading from the crimes right to Glick. Although the investigations into the two homicides did not yield any convictions, Tony Spilotro was widely believed to have been the man behind them. Tony was invariably associated with Lefty Rosenthal in the media, and Lefty in turn was tied to Glick at the Stardust. The implication was that Glick may have been the one giving orders, meaning he would be one of the higher-ups in the supposed criminal organization. This is exactly what the mobsters out East that backed him wanted to avoid.

The Civella Family that reigned in Kansas City actually wanted to remove Glick from the organization altogether. They had long considered him a pestering nuisance because of his resistance to the takeover, but after the Rand and Buccieri murder investigations, he became a major liability. The Civellas wanted to either force him out of the casinos, or potentially force him to "buy out" the Family, but for this they would have expected an absolute fortune. When the Kansas City Family discovered Glick was also embezzling his loan payments, they were even more furious, and would have preferred just to kill him. In 1977, future Kansas City boss Carl Cevilla began plotting against him alongside the Family's underboss, Carl DeLuna. The two high-ranking mobsters even flew around the country meeting with the leaders of other Families in the Midwest and elsewhere, trying to get a consensus on what should be done to remove Allen Glick. In 1978, the pair met with Milwaukee boss Frank Balistrieri, as well as Turk Torrello, Jackie Cerone, and Joe Aiuppa of Chicago, to try to settle it once and for all. Many possibilities were suggested and DeLuna, who had a tendency to take extensive notes, kept a close record of all of them. It's not shocking that this turned out to be a disastrous mistake, as it left a strong line of physical evidence for investigators.

While Glick's enemies were making moves and plotting his downfall, he remained intransigent. For years he had accepted the fact that his company was going to be at least partially controlled by others. But it was still *his* company, and he was steadfast on that point. He was not going to meet their huge cash demands to get them to leave his casinos alone, and he certainly wasn't prepared to give up his position in the Argent Corporation. The Families were getting impatient. Glick was eventually called to a meeting with DeLuna that took place in the office of Mr. Oscar Goodman, who often allowed his mobster clients to use the space for private meetings. At this meeting, the capo from Kansas City used his most aggressive tactic yet. Since Glick clearly had no regard for his own life, given his continued refusal to exit the business, the Civella Family was instead threatening to murder Glick's children. If he did not remove himself from the operation of the Stardust, Hacienda, Marina, and Fremont casinos, DeLuna would personally see to it that both of his sons, Todd and Cary, were killed. Glick obviously thought that DeLuna wasn't joking. Within just a few days of his warning, Glick went to the Gaming Commission and informed them of his intention to sell his gambling operations.

So, at least the Civella Family had got what they wanted, and Glick was soon to be a distant memory. Unfortunately, in 1978, the situation surrounding Argent became nightmarish. That year, the FBI had successfully planted listening devices in a local Kansas City pizza parlor named Villa Capri. It was long considered a likely mob hangout by the FBI, and the wiretaps were originally placed to try to gather information on a recent murder that they believed was Mafia related. They heard a lot of incriminating conversations, but none were about their murder. Instead, what they overheard was Carl DeLuna and Carl Civella discussing their illegal casino operations. They talked about their method of purchasing them, and they described how they had coerced Allen Glick into leaving the company under threat, though the sale of the casinos was not yet official. Just eight days after the federal agents heard this conversation though, Glick announced publicly that he was going to be leaving his position in Argent, which confirmed the story that the FBI overheard. Unfortunately for Lefty's partners, DeLuna and Civella also brought up the Chicago Outfit's de facto ownership of the Stardust and others, implicating them as well. This was a major and unexpected breakthrough for the FBI, as it was the first time the Midwest Families were caught openly talking about their role in the gaming industry. Due to a combination of DeLuna's extensive notes which were later confiscated by federal agents and the wiretaps in both the Villa Capri and in the Gold Rush, the FBI now had solid evidence of the long-suspected link between the Las Vegas Strip, the Midwest Mafia Families, and the Teamsters. By 1979, due to pressure from both the Mafia and the law, Glick was fully forced out of the casino business.

The 1981 El Dorado

By the new decade, Lefty and Geri's relationship reached a tipping point. In 1980, Geri began having frequent, significant mental breakdowns. Likely as a result of both her drug abuse and her severe dissatisfaction with her marriage, she could barely function normally anymore. Lefty, too, had very little love left for the woman that had captured his heart years earlier at the Tropicana. She had tried to steal his children from him, and she had fought him almost constantly for years. She took everything she could from Lefty, but she gave very little back. She was driven into Tony's arms, and their affair just further convinced her that she deserved better than Lefty. One day, when Geri was in one of her fits of violent rage, she called the police and falsely reported that her home was being robbed. When the cops arrived, they instead found Geri outside, holding a loaded handgun, threatening to murder her husband, Lefty. The police tried in vain to talk her down before she decided she wanted to leave. She somehow convinced the officers to escort her to the bank that Lefty had some of his larger accounts at and stand guard as she emptied several of her husband's safety deposit boxes, clearing out nearly a half million dollars in cash plus another million in jewelry and gems. Then, Geri took off, never to return. Just three days later, Lefty officially filed for divorce, and his marriage to Geri came to an ignominious end.

In 1978, Tony finally reaped the consequences of his greed. His delusions of grandeur and his desire to conquer the city of Las Vegas were finally made clear to the Outfit bosses after they discovered that he had been double skimming from the same casinos he was sent there to protect. He had been pocketing cash from the original skim that was destined to be flown out East and keeping it for himself. Since it was already cash that was off the books, he thought neither the Stardust, its auditors, nor the bosses would know that the money was being pilfered. He was wrong. After the discovery of his double skim somehow came to light, both Lefty and the bosses were furious with Tony, and he had become as much of a nuisance as Lefty had been with his television show. But Tony's greed extended to more than just money. He took whatever he wanted, and one of the things he wanted was Geri Rosenthal. Before Geri disappeared from the city, rumors swirled around Vegas about her and Tony's relationship, and when these rumors reached Chicago, the bosses were furious. How could they trust Tony's impulse control when he screwed around on the same guy he was supposed to be protecting? Even if Lefty was becoming an annoyance himself, ruining his marriage was too far and it was sure to cause even more discord in their Vegas operations. What had once been a shining jewel of profit for the Outfit was quickly becoming a flaming heap of trouble.

Heading into the 1980s, Tony's position was tenuous at best. He had pissed off all the wrong people, and after a streak of botched robberies and heists, as well as several accidental murders committed by members of his crew, things were starting to look very grim for the Hole in the Wall Gang and the self-proclaimed boss of Las Vegas. Lefty was also facing his biggest setback yet. In the late 1970s, just about all of his involvement in the casino industry came to a screeching halt when the Gaming Control Board demanded that Lefty Rosenthal, despite being only an Entertainment Director, *still* needed to obtain a gaming license to operate in his role at the Stardust. Lefty wasn't the only one. The

Board also came for Joe Agosto, who was also an Entertainment Director and representative of the Civella Family. Earlier, Agosto had clearly told his bosses that Lefty was going to bring heat on everybody and that his presence in Vegas put all of their operations at risk. Clearly, Agosto's prediction was accurate, and Lefty had directly disrupted the Kansas City Mafia's casino business. This decision from the Board was essentially a death sentence for both of their careers, as neither stood any chance of actually acquiring a license. Barred from holding any position of significance at the Stardust, Lefty was now effectively forced out of the Las Vegas Strip. Like his marriage just a few years later, Lefty's years-long public battle with Nevada's gaming authorities had ended in a humiliating defeat.

After Lefty was pushed out, he still remained in the city. His casino career may have been over, but he was dedicated to the art of gambling, and he eventually just went back to his old sports betting ways, handicapping and studying the odds to make a living. He was doing what he loved, but his life was certainly a lot less exciting. Eventually he fell into quite a rigid routine, waking at the same time every day, going to the same places, and doing the same things. The only thing that changed was which games he was going to be placing wagers on that day. This strict and predictable daily schedule proved to be a nearly fatal mistake, as it made him a very easy man to find, and the many enemies he had made for himself over the years apparently were keeping their eyes open. In October of 1982, as Lefty was leaving Tony Roma's restaurant on East Sahara Avenue, which he dined at nearly every single day, an attempt was made on his life. As he got back into his car with his takeout order, he turned the ignition and heard an unusual sound. Starting the engine of his 1981 Cadillac El Dorado actually triggered the activation of a bomb hidden on the underside of the car. Before the explosion, smoke began fuming out of the hood, and the only thing going through Lefty's mind was "why is my car on fire?" (quoted in Pileggi, 1995). Before he had a chance to collect his thoughts and react appropriately, a sudden explosion threw him from the car and onto the pavement outside. The initial blast nearly broke his ribs, and despite being covered in flames, he survived with minimal injuries. As he rolled around trying to snuff out the flames, people rushed over to help him. Then, the gas tank ignited causing a second, larger explosion that sent his El Dorado straight up in the air in a plume of smoke and flame.

Lefty survived the assassination attempt, but he was far from safe. Someone clearly wanted him dead, and they were obviously more than capable of reaching him. To make things more complicated, there was no telling who was behind it. Indeed, whoever was behind the explosion remains a mystery to this day, but there are a few likely possibilities. The first is Tony Spilotro. Tony, by this point, hated Lefty. He had slept with his wife, who was then driven out of the city, and he viewed Lefty's status with a lot of resentment. He saw him as the reason that their golden age in Las Vegas came to a crashing end and blamed him fully for angering the bosses. The second possibility was none other than Geri Rosenthal, his now ex-wife. Geri had a seething hatred for Lefty and even if she wasn't behind it, she very likely would have wanted him dead anyway. After Geri made off with Lefty's cash and jewelry, she fled back home to Southern California. Back home, Geri had many close friends that were members of violent and notorious biker gangs, and it wouldn't be at all shocking if she had either convinced them or paid them to kill Lefty while in a drunken or drug induced rage. She very likely told them plenty of stories about Lefty's cruelty, both real and exaggerated, and it's also possible they took it upon themselves to make a trip to Nevada to plant the bomb as a favor to her. The third and possibly most likely culprits, however, were the Midwest gangsters. The order could have come down from the bosses of the Chicago Outfit, likely as retribution for his years of costly antics. The order also could have come from an external Family, possibly the Civellas in Kansas City. Most of the evidence, though, points to Frank Balistrieri, the boss of Milwaukee and Lefty's former supporter. Balistrieri reportedly blamed Lefty for the Outfit deciding to cut him out of his share of the casino earnings, and given the Milwaukee Family's significant presence in Vegas, it's certainly possible it was Balistrieri's men that planted the bomb.

Regardless of who the culprit was, Lefty's luck obviously hadn't run out quite yet. He survived a horrific explosion that by all means should have killed him. Actually, the only reason he did survive was because of the car he drove. The 1981 model of the Cadillac El Dorado happened to have a manufacturing defect that was only discovered after the line was finished production. The defect caused an imbalance in the car between the driver's and passenger's side, which affected the car's drivability. To correct this, the manufacturer placed a thick metal sheet under the driver's seat in all the cars coming off the assembly line to add some weight to that side. Luckily for Lefty, this same sheet acted as a barrier between Lefty and the blast, which came from the underside of the car. If Lefty had been driving just about any other car, he almost certainly would have died that day. Despite Lefty's belief that luck played no role in his life, it's hard to attribute his survival to anything else. Not everyone could be as lucky as him though.

The lives of nearly everyone that Lefty had associated with were coming crashing down around him. In November of 1982, Geri Rosenthal was found unresponsive in a California motel room that she had been living in. She was quickly declared dead, apparently having suffered complications from a lethal drug overdose. Then, in September of 1983, a total of 15 high-ranking mobsters from the Midwest received indictments from a grand jury in Kansas City, stemming from the skim operation in the case against the Argent Corporation. The list of those indicted contained a lot of big names, including current Chicago Outfit boss Joey Aiuppa as well as underlings Jackie Cerone and Joey Lombardo. In December, Lombardo and Teamsters President Roy Williams were both convicted of bribery of a Nevada State Senator, and in 1986, Lombardo was also convicted in the skimming case, receiving 10 years for that sentence. Also convicted in 1986 were Auippa, who received a whopping 28-year sentence, as well as Kansas City gangsters Carl Civella and Carl DeLuna, who each received 10 to 20 years, and Civella's son, Anthony. Tony Spilotro was also indicted, but his fate would be much different.

That particular indictment was only the most recent of Tony Spilotro's legal troubles. Around the same time, Tony was involved in another felony case centered on the 1981 attempted robbery of a luxury furniture store called Bertha's, which happened to be on the same road as the Gold Rush. The robbery itself actually went smoothly, but unfortunately for the Hole in the Wall Gang, it was doomed from the start. One of their crew members, a crook named

Sal Romano, had been picked up by the feds earlier and was successfully flipped, becoming an informant for law enforcement. He was involved in the planning stage of the Bertha's robbery and tipped off the cops in advance. The police knew exactly who was going to be there, and when. When they crashed the party, it looked like it might be the end for Tony's entire crew. A bunch of the guys involved got pinched, and one of them was Tony's right-hand man and lifelong friend from Chicago, Frank Cullotta. This arrest had serious, life altering consequences.

When Frank Cullotta was being held and spoken to by the police after the Bertha's incident, they seemed to have formed some kind of rapport. The police identified Cullotta as a potential person of interest, and sure enough, a few months after the bust, Cullotta was approached and picked up again by FBI agent Charlie Parsons. He said he had something he needed to show Frank. Parsons revealed to Frank that Tony's establishments, including the Gold Rush, had been thoroughly bugged by his team. They had heard a lot of interesting things, but one conversation in particular was especially relevant to Frank. The agents played the recording for Frank, who was now intrigued and curious. It was of a phone call between Tony and Joey Lombardo, who was back home in Chicago. In it, Tony explicitly requests permission from Lombardo to whack a guy in Las Vegas who had apparently been causing Tony some trouble. The portion that Parsons showed Frank did not reveal the name of the man Tony was referring to, but it was clear enough to him. He was talking about Frank. Perhaps it was because Tony blamed him for the several botched robberies, or because he simply didn't trust Cullotta anymore. Whatever his reasons, Frank now felt betrayed and afraid for his life. Shortly after, Frank decided to flip. He began co-operating with the FBI and started spying and informing on Tony Spilotro. He later also became a willing state witness. The loss of Frank Cullotta to the government was one of the biggest blows to strike Tony and the Hole in the Wall Gang, as Cullotta had power and connections of his own. Eventually, Cullotta was sent into protective custody for his role.

Later in 1983, more indictments were handed down during the Bertha's case. They included many top dogs in Vegas, including Tony Spilotro himself, his younger brother Michael, Tony's Gold Rush partner Fat Herb Blitzstein, as well as most of the core crew of the Hole in the Wall Gang. Frank Cullotta was already proving himself to be a lethal weapon for the FBI, as the majority of these indictments were directly based on his co-operation and testimonials. The trial for these charges was set to begin in 1985 but later got postponed because the huge Argent case, which handed down convictions for skimming roughly $2 million in casino profits, was taking place at the same time. When the Argent case was concluded, the Outfit leadership, now devoid of Joey Aiuppa, Angelo LaPietra, and Jackie Cerone, was decimated. The Kansas City Family was struck too, having lost the likes of Carl DeLuna. The involvement of Joe Agosto, the former Tropicana Entertainment Director who had turned government witness alongside Frank Cullotta, helped ensure that the Kansas City gangsters didn't get off unscathed. Even worse than the lost talent was the fact that the Midwest Families had now almost completely lost access to their biggest moneymaker ever, the Las Vegas casinos. Blame for this shattering tragedy was placed firmly at the feet of Frank "Lefty" Rosenthal and Tony "the Ant" Spilotro, the two people whose job it was to protect the skim and to avoid undue attention from the police. Clearly, they failed spectacularly in both of these goals. While they were not directly responsible for the Argent case, these two guys had steadily transformed Vegas' landscape into one that welcomed, even invited the eyes of the government and police.

The Bertha's trial and Argent case promised to finally hand down justice to Tony for his role in the Las Vegas crime spree that began when Tony formed the Hole in the Wall Gang. The original Bertha's case ended in a mistrial after it was discovered that bribery was playing a role in the jury stand, and a new date was set to try again. However, one week before the second trial was slated to begin, Tony and his brother Michael went missing. As it turns out, the pair was called back to Chicago in June of 1986 for a meeting with the top brass to discuss what their next steps should be, and to determine the Family's future plans in Nevada. They never returned, and no one had seen them since. A hunt for the two brothers began, and some believed they may have fled the country to avoid prosecution. But the two were eventually found not too far from home, buried in a large field in Indiana. When they were uncovered, their bodies were severely bruised and bloody, and it was clear they had both been beaten to death as retribution. The powers that be had had enough of Tony and his penchant for spectacular crimes and stealing from his bosses. The Las Vegas skim was now over forever, and so was the violent reign of Tony "the Ant" Spilotro.

Spilotro's murder may have been necessary, but unfortunately for the Chicago Outfit, it just made things worse. After he was found murdered, several Outfit guys operating in Vegas who were in the middle of indictments and trials began to flip and become state witnesses. Clearly, someone in a powerful position had decided it was time to clean house. They worried that Tony and Michael Spilotro were just the beginning, and that they wouldn't think twice about murdering more if they believed they posed a threat during trial. If they agreed to tell the FBI and prosecutors what they wanted to know, they would at least have government protection to hide behind. This led to the exposure of even more of the Mafia's secrets in Las Vegas and further crippled the mob's presence in the city. Tony Spilotro was dead. His right-hand man Frank Cullotta forsook a life of crime and was now working with the government to uncover criminal influence. All of the Outfit's casinos (as well as those of the Kansas City and Milwaukee Families) were being scoured and having their records gone through with a fine-tooth comb by federal agents and gaming regulations authorities. Their leaders were staring down the barrel of a decade-long prison sentence, if not more. The only variable that seemed to have avoided the chaos and legal circus was Lefty.

Lefty's time in Las Vegas had already been disrupted by the end of 1983. That year, the Stardust as a whole had its license fully suspended as the FBI launched yet another probing investigation into the criminal activity that had been allegedly taking place there since the early 1970s. At the time, there was still some disjointed and scattered Mafia presence within the casino, but Nevada and federal authorities had basically moved right into the building. While there they began to clean house, eliminating all trace elements of criminal influence. They terminated any and all employees that they believed may have been involved in some capacity with the skimming operation, even if they were just found to be complicit. This completely changed the structure of the Stardust casino and made it virtually impossible for the Outfit to recover their chokehold on the establishment. The grand, luxurious office space that Lefty had built for himself within the casino had now been commandeered and repurposed as a headquarters for a supervisor from the Gaming Control Board who had been placed there to monitor the Stardust.

Lefty didn't stick around for the entire mess. Less than a year after the attempt on his life was made outside Tony Roma's restaurant, Lefty packed up and left Vegas for California. Lefty of course brought his children along, who stayed with him after their mother abandoned them for a life of narcotics in a rundown Southern California motel room, and the family settled in a city called Laguna Niguel in Orange County. Laguna Niguel was another fresh start for Lefty, but he also had his children in mind. Since their time in Vegas, his kids had become very talented competitive swimmers, and Laguna Niguel was home to the Mission Viejo Nadadores, one of the most elite swim teams in the entire nation, and since Lefty had Olympic dreams for his kids, he wanted them to be able to train there with the best.

As for Lefty himself, he once again went back to his old gambling habits, betting on games that he was especially confident about and earning a living off his picks. Later in life he also took his talents to the stock market, becoming a day trader and using his skilled analyses to predict surefire corporate winners. It seems he found some success in his new life, and later moved to Florida again and took up residence in the beautiful resort city of Boca Raton, where he operated a sports bar called Crocs. He even ran a sports betting website at www.frankrosenthal.com where gamblers could see Lefty's picks and get his advice on big games. In October of 2008, at the age of 79, Frank "Lefty" Rosenthal died. He had become one of the most visionary and revolutionary figures in the history of Las Vegas, and his lasting influence can still be found on casino floors to this day. Though he had fought a losing battle since he stepped foot in the city, Las Vegas still has not forgotten him. The game was rigged against him from the start, and although Lefty was the man who always seemed to beat the odds, his luck had to run out sometime.

CONCLUSION
CODENAME ACHILLES

For the remainder of Lefty's life, he stayed far away from the Las Vegas casino scene. This, however, was not necessarily by choice. While Lefty was in California, shortly after leaving Las Vegas, the state of Nevada officially blacklisted him, banning him from every gambling establishment in the state. Lefty did contest the ban, as he obviously wasn't ready to walk away from casinos forever, but the Nevada Supreme Court eventually stepped in to quash the appeal and uphold his lifetime prohibition. Still, nothing could keep him from gambling, which is what he spent the majority of the rest of his days doing in Florida. It seems, though, that Lefty really did get off easy, at least in comparison to his former partners who were almost all either in prison, in witness protection, or in the ground. So, the question remains, how the hell was Lefty allowed to retire in the first place? Indeed, Lefty's ability to get off scot-free was a mystery for decades. To outside observers, he must have seemed like the luckiest guy to ever live, but in reality, luck could not have had less to do with it. Lefty knew exactly why he was able to move out of Nevada without the lingering threat of prosecution looming over him and without ever having to defend himself against the skimming charges which took place within the very casinos that he operated. But he was one of just a handful of people in the world that did know. That is, until he died.

Lefty was a born gambler, and it was in his nature to always consider what might happen if he lost. How could he protect himself in case he made a bad bet? What if his horse actually lost? Just weeks after his death in October of 2008, news broke that Lefty Rosenthal was, in fact, an informant for the FBI and had been for many years. His codename in the FBI was "Achilles," likely a reference to the fact that having him was like having the "Achilles' Heel" of the Chicago Mafia and their Vegas business. This wasn't exactly surprising news. After his stint in Vegas was over, many in the mob world, both the ones who remained free and the ones that were now locked up, wondered whether Lefty was feeding the cops info from the inside. It would have certainly explained a lot, but Lefty was always insistent that he would never be a rat. It just wasn't in his character. Even when he was the flashy host of *The Frank Rosenthal Show*, he was still a Chicago kid at heart. He was from the West Side, and the same guys he worked with were the guys he grew up with. On top of this, Oscar Goodman, the mob lawyer who often represented Lefty and served as his counsel always insisted that he would never represent an informant or someone who betrayed their friends. He simply didn't allow his clients to flip. Nevertheless, almost immediately after Lefty's death, three individual law enforcement officials came forward with their stories about the real Lefty Rosenthal.

According to the Las Vegas Review-Journal, Lefty wasn't just an average rat, but a so-called "top echelon" informant who had some of the most valuable information available from within the Mafia structure (Morrison, 2008). It's even more impressive, then, that his secret identity managed to remain a secret for so long. For their part, his FBI handlers never exposed who he was because they genuinely didn't want Lefty to get assassinated by the Mafia in retribution. Once he was dead though, there was nothing stopping the men from coming forward to share their stories. When they did, it revealed the true extent of Lefty's treachery. It's not known exactly how long Lefty had been informing on his colleagues, but it was much longer than one might suspect. One might assume that he would have run to federal agents for protection immediately after his car exploded in the early 1980s, but actually, Lefty was already a seasoned veteran in ratting by the time this happened. In fact, after the bombing of his car, his handlers tried to convince him to relocate and move into witness protection officially because they feared he had somehow been exposed as an informant, but Lefty categorically refused.

For years, Lefty always made a big deal about how badly the FBI wanted to flip him and he would tell stories of his absolute defiance in the face of their bribes. He said they offered him almost total immunity in return for access to what he knew, but he said he always turned them down. In the late 1970s, he claimed that he was being harassed and targeted by FBI agents because they were angry that he refused to co-operate with them. He even claimed that as far back as his time in Miami, the FBI Director J. Edgar Hoover himself sent a squad of agents to request his co-operation on the state of organized gambling across the entire United States of America. Lefty said that Hoover's men offered him nearly everything under the sun just to be able to pick his brain. Most likely, this was just a way for Lefty to massage his ego while also diverting attention away from him, because as he said, he still outright refused to help the law. Even much later in his life, he always claimed that snitching just wasn't in his blood. It wasn't who he was. However, knowing what we know about Lefty, this isn't quite true. Actually, snitching would have been very in character for someone like him. A lifelong gambling man, Lefty was a guy who hedged his bets. Knowing that the only thing that could protect him once his scams ran out was the cops themselves, lending the FBI his knowledge every once in a while, was his way of hedging the most important bet of his life.

All signs point to Lefty having been at least an occasional informant for the cops since his time back in Chicago originally. This means that from his hometown, to Miami, back to Chicago, and finally to Las Vegas, Lefty allowed the FBI to keep tabs on the Outfit operations the entire time. Although Lefty never once testified against the Mafia as a whole, nor against any of his associates, but he certainly helped put some of them behind bars. Even in this realm, Lefty walked a tightrope. He needed to give the feds enough information that they would continue to protect him and stay off his back, but he couldn't give away so much that it would damage his business or make any of his bosses suspicious of him. Similar to how he had spent years mastering the craft of odds making, designing wagers that were both highly enticing to gamblers while also guaranteeing he got the largest payout, Lefty also had to balance his work with the FBI with his work for the mob. All of it needed to be perfect and given the fact that nobody knew for sure whether Lefty was snitching until decades after his Las Vegas career, he at least succeeded in this area. He always kept the FBI within arm's reach, offering up valuable pieces of information while withholding anything that would be too catastrophic. Amazingly, even in this position, Lefty seemed to be in total control.

So, with the end of the Lefty Rosenthal and Tony Spilotro eras in Las Vegas, so ended the era of the Mafia dominating Sin City. The pair of Chicago gangsters were handed everything they could have ever wanted, but instead, they burned it all to the ground. Lefty with his ego and stubbornness, and Tony with his greed and recklessness turned what used to be a quiet but profitable money machine into a hotspot for violent crime and federal investigations. The city where criminals of all stripes used to be able to operate peacefully and safely during the 1960s and early 1970s had been morphed into a Medieval kingdom where Tony Spilotro reigned alone as monarch. It was a city where the police used to be easily plied with bribes and favors, but they were now partnering with federal agents to cripple organized crime in the city permanently. The duo's arrival coincided with a significant spike in the rate of violent crimes, and all of a sudden, even small-time criminals began finding it difficult to operate in the city without kicking up a tribute in some way to Tony Spilotro. His years-long chain of break-ins and robberies, both successful and horribly botched, brought unprecedented heat down on the city and caused significant strife between the various Mafia Families that shared the marketplace of Las Vegas crime. And because Lefty could not escape his life-long connection with Tony, his reputation was dragged through the mud right alongside him.

After Lefty and Tony were out of the picture, the Outfit tried to maintain whatever influence it had left. In 1986, Tony was replaced as the top enforcer in Vegas by Donald Angelini (the same Donald Angelini of Angel-Kaplan, the betting group Lefty had worked for so many years ago), who tried desperately to provide new avenues of income as the Stardust and their other flagship resorts were being strangled by the FBI and tax authorities. His efforts were doomed from the start, however. He had attempted to expand the Outfit's waning influence out West by making a move on the Rincon Indian Reservation casino in San Diego in the late 1980s. As a reward for his efforts in strong-arming the casino, however, all Angelini received was a three year prison sentence for racketeering. It was clear enough that their control over the Las Vegas Strip had been destroyed, and with that, they also began losing control over their street rackets like prostitution, robberies, and drug trafficking. Some of their most reliable moneymakers, like loan shark Herbie Blitzstein (Tony's former partner at the Gold Rush jewelry shop) were gunned down in later years, removing yet another member from the old school Vegas crew.

Not everyone made out quite so bad, though. Frank Cullotta, for example, was placed in Witness Protection and after he served his time, he was a free man. Cullotta later became involved in the "tourist" aspect of Mafia life, giving tours of Mafia hangouts and authoring books about his experiences from the inside. Cullotta certainly embraced his past, but he lived out the rest of his life as a free man and never returned to a life of crime. Oscar Goodman, the long-time Mafia advisor and close associate of Lefty, Tony, and Frank Cullotta among others, is another case in point. In 1999, Goodman translated a successful legal career into a political one, being elected Mayor of Las Vegas. Surprisingly, Goodman didn't seem to try to downplay the involvement of organized crime in his beloved city of Las Vegas (he was actually from Philadelphia). In fact, in an era when "Mob Vegas" was a mere thing of the past, Goodman actually cleverly used it as a tourist draw. He promoted sites around the city as attractions that would bring in organized crime enthusiasts from all over the country and also provide some history to those who just wanted a break from the blackjack tables.

The way Cullotta and Goodman approached their Mafia pasts is actually quite fitting for the new era that Las Vegas found itself in. After the age of Rosenthal and Spilotro, Las Vegas was a completely changed city. On the outside, it was still all flashy neon lights and towering casino hotels and huge, beautiful marquis signs, but on the inside and down on the street, it was another beast. The gangsters that controlled the floors were gone and the glittery aura of high-life luxury was also, for the most part, gone. Las Vegas was no longer a haven for big-time gamers and degenerates alike. It was more like a theme park, with large corporations moving in to replace the old shady Mafia structures. Sin City had become a corporate paradise that functioned much more like a vacation resort than a gambling mecca. Las Vegas became warm and family-friendly, a place where respectable, decent people come for vacation, feel safe and secure, and bet a couple dollars at the penny slots before heading to the buffet or the myriads of tourist attractions. All of Lefty's innovations remained ingrained into the fabric of Las Vegas casinos, but the high rollers were replaced by middle-class folks who were looking for some low stakes card games or maybe bingo. With Lefty's pals gone and big business moving into town, Las Vegas became Disney World in the desert. Las Vegas still remained the gambling capital of the country, but for those chasing the high stakes thrills of the city's nightlife and casino scenes, it simply was not the same town.

When it came to blame for the downfall of the Mafia in Las Vegas, it might be an exaggeration to say it all lies at the feet of Lefty

Rosenthal and Tony Spilotro. Still, the impact these two had on the city was irreparable, and there's no doubt that their influence was monumental in what Las Vegas became. According to Frank Cullotta, Tony's behavior was possibly the sole cause of the end of Outfit Vegas: "Tony had been the Outfit's man in Vegas. He had the world by the balls but had fucked it all up with unauthorized hits, botched robberies, and an affair with Lefty's wife," (Cullotta, 2017). It was, however, Lefty's insistence on publicly calling out the Gaming Commission and Control Board that made it impossible for the authorities to continue ignoring Vegas. For many people, Lefty had made the fight personal, and it was never one he could win in the first place. Still, the Las Vegas of the 1970s remains one of the most fabled periods in American history, and for better or worse, the story of the Las Vegas Strip remains one of the most epic sagas in the history of the Italian-American Mafia.

REFERENCES

A judge refused Wednesday to dismiss murder charges against... (1983, October 26). UPI. https://www.upi.com/Archives/1983/10/26/A-judge-refused-Wednesday-to-dismiss-murder-charges-against/8118435988800/

Bonesteel, M. (2022, August 29). *Sports betting timeline: From Las Vegas to the Supreme Court.* The Washington Post. https://www.washingtonpost.com/sports/2022/08/29/history-of-sports-gambling/

Carlock, R. (n.d.). *Lefty Rosenthal: King of Vegas or informant extraordinaire?* History Defined. https://www.historydefined.net/lefty-rosenthal/

Chepesiuk, R. (2010). *Gangsters of Miami: True tales of mobsters, gamblers, hitmen, con men, and gang bangers from the Magic City.* Barricade Books.

CRIME: It pays to organize. (1951, March 12). TIME. https://content.time.com/time/subscriber/article/0,33009,805815-7,00.html

Cullotta, F. (2017). *The rise and fall of a 'Casino' mobster: The Tony Spilotro story through a hitman's eyes.* WildBlue Press.

German, J. (2019, October 21). *The mafia's history in Las Vegas: From Bugsy Siegel to Anthony Spilotro.* Las Vegas Review-Journal. https://www.reviewjournal.com/local/local-las-vegas/the-mafias-history-in-las-vegas-from-bugsy-siegel-to-anthony-spilotro-413833/

Griffin, D. (2006). *The battle for Las Vegas: The law vs. the mob.* Huntington Press.

Henry, L. (2021, August 7). *Allen Glick, 1970s owner of Las Vegas casinos skimmed by mob, has died.* Mob Museum. https://themobmuseum.org/blog/allen-glick-1970s-owner-of-las-vegas-casinos-skimmed-by-mob-has-died/

Matheson, V. (2021). "An overview of the economics of sports gambling and an introduction to the symposium." *East Econ Journal* 47(1), 1-8. https://www.ncbi.nlm.nih.gov/pmc/articles/PMC7780080/

Maverick, J.B. (2023, September 18). *Why does the house always win? A look at casino profitability.* Investopedia. https://www.investopedia.com/articles/personal-finance/110415/why-does-house-always-win-look-casino-profitability.asp

Moe, A. (2022). *Vegas and the Chicago Outfit: The skimming of Las Vegas.* Self-published.

Morrison, J. A. (2008, October 30). *'Lefty' Rosenthal was an FBI snitch.* Las Vegas Review-Journal. https://www.reviewjournal.com/news/news-columns/jane-ann-morrison/lefty-rosenthal-was-an-fbi-snitch/

Pileggi, N. (1995). *Casino: Love and honor in Las Vegas.* Open Road.

Redd, W. (2022, November 28). *Frank Rosenthal and the real story of Sam Rothstein from 'Casino.'* AllThatsInteresting. https://allthatsinteresting.com/frank-rosenthal

www.ingramcontent.com/pod-product-compliance
Lightning Source LLC
Chambersburg PA
CBHW072055110526
44590CB00018B/3178